The Lost Letters

The Lost Letters

The Dark World of Narcissistic Abuse

E A CARTER

Arundel House Press

Award-winning fiction by E A Carter
The Lost Valor of Love
The Call of Eternity
The Rise of the Goddess
I, Cassandra

Copyright © 2021 by E A CARTER

The moral right of the author is hereby asserted in accordance with the Copyright, Designs and Patents Act 1988

Although this publication is designed to provide accurate information in regard to the subject matter covered, the publisher and the author assume no responsibility for errors, inaccuracies, omissions, or any other inconsistencies herein.

This publication is meant as a source of valuable information for the reader, however it is not meant as a replacement for direct expert assistance. If such level of assistance is required, the services of a competent professional should be sought.

Some names and identifying details of people described in this book have been altered to protect their privacy.

All rights reserved. No part of this publication may be reproduced, stored in a retrieval system, or transmitted, in any form or by any means without the prior written permission of the publisher, nor be otherwise circulated in any form of binding or cover other than that in which it is published and without a similar condition being imposed on the subsequent buyer.

First Edition
Printed in the United Kingdom
First Printing, 2022
ISBN 978-1-7399325-2-7
Arundel House Press www.arundelhousepress.com

For M,
Who wouldn't let me go.

It began with the chase,
persistent and light.
She fell to his grace,
his charm, and his might.
He said he loved her
but there was always
a price.
Impossible rules
that controlled
her life.
He took her space, her air,
her voice, her sight.
Imprisoned her in his
World of endless night.
He dined on her love,
her soul, and her light.
Gorged on her fear,
her pain, her hope.
Her plight.
And when he was done.
He told her the lie.
It was she who was evil,
and he the knight.
Elizabeth Anne Carter

A TESTAMENT OF A LIE

It began with a lie, as all things too good to be true tend to do.

Eleven and a half years later, I hide in the south of Poland, rapidly going bankrupt from fighting an endless court battle against a man who is using his wealth and nepotist connections to ensure I am left with nothing. And in this place where my ears are blind and my eyes are drowning in rustic beauty, I sit before my beloved keyboard and write a testament of hell. Of destruction. Of evil.

Of the silent, insidious process of someone systematically eradicating the identity, self, worth and value of another with escalating psychological, financial, sexual, and physical abuse.

It takes a special type of personality to possess the lack of empathy required to hijack a person's love and trust and use it to invalidate them, punish them, and turn their heart into weapon to be used against them. To control them.

Narcissists are everywhere. They live among us. Hard to spot. Harder to catch. Impossible to stop. They enter your life with calculation and expertise, are excellent listeners (at the beginning), because information is power. Their story is always the same. They are the victim of selfish people who have taken advantage of their generosity and goodness. They prey on your empathy, sharing their tale of woe until you are seduced by their words, and of how incredibly fortunate you are that they appear to be the very one you have been waiting for. You know you won't do to them what their previous partner did. You know you are perfect for them. They tell you they love you. You fall. Hard. And they are there to catch you.

Perhaps you get two months. Perhaps a year. It is a fairytale. A love affair drenched in passion, adventure, and excitement. You can't believe your luck. They ask you to marry them.

You say yes. You don't want them to slip away.

And then the fairytale ends. Like the proverbial frog in the frying pan, things shift subtly. At first you express concerns. You are told you are over-reacting. Doubt plagues you. Not about *them*—about your ability to see things as they truly are. Nothing is clear. You try to get clarity so you carefully frame your question. It's not right. You try again. Still not right. You are corrected. Often. Gently, with a smile, as though you are cute but a little dense. Something feels off. You used to be able to trust your gut. Not anymore. It seems your gut is the liar these days. Soon you give up saying what you see or remember because you never get it right and have to be corrected. It's just easier to let them tell you how it is. How that blind woman with the seeing eye dog *wasn't* on the pedestrian crossing and your partner almost ran them over. You saw it wrong. They weren't even on the crossing.

But you saw the dog almost get hit.

Or did you?

As your light dies from their continual crises, drama, and fights created out of thin air, a line is crossed. Exhausted of your internal energy, of your light, of what made you who you are, you become a shell, no longer of any use or interest to your once-fairytale partner. Now you are looked at with derision. The hate begins. And it's terrifying. Like an abused dog who knows nothing better, you crawl back, trying to appease them, to please them, to get the fairytale days back. To get the hate to stop. Because if they hate you, you must also hate yourself. The pain is unbearable.

Sometimes they relent and are kind for a day, maybe a week, or even a month. It's an oasis of heaven in the midst of a burning hell . . . but then the pendulum swings back and the hate returns again, the treatment even worse than before.

Over and over the pattern repeats until in desperation you have no choice but to turn against your Self, make your thoughts and experiences wrong and theirs right, and accept that everything—everything—is your fault. Caught in their riptide, your existence is slammed against the sharp rocks of their bleak shore, and the only way to end the storm (they tell you) is to do what they ask, but each time the request is more humiliating, demeaning, and annihilating . . . until you are not you anymore, but a broken thing, lost, isolated, and trapped in the glare of their intense, insatiable hatred.

One year ago yesterday, the divorce was finalized. But the court fight goes on. He claims I owe him money for having supported me. I had no job. I had nothing. It was how he wanted it. Now he wants not only everything there is from the marriage, but he also wishes to put me into debt to him. I have gathered up the scraps of the fight that remains within me to write this for you. If only someone had written this book before I met him, if only someone had recommended it to me. How different my life might be right now. Perhaps I might not have seen through the fantasy he created at the beginning, but I would have understood sooner what he was, and *why* he was doing what he was doing, and how it would never, ever end until either I died, or was discarded, a broken, ruined woman. I would not have continued on in the false hope that somehow I could make things better.

But there was no book, and back then no one really knew or talked much about narcissists, so I was unprepared for the enormity of the sacrifice my heart had made in its pursuit of a love that was a complete lie.

My story is ugly, painful, and at times, utterly brutal. When others hear the recordings of what I endured, they cry, even the men weep. It will be hard to write this. I will be forced to relive awful memories. But after months of consideration, and the encouragement of my friends, I know I cannot remain silent when I have the gift of words and the knowledge this experience has given me. My father says the greatest thing one can do is to give service to others. Perhaps I was always meant to write this book, even if it has come to cost me almost everything. Perhaps as I sit here in the ruins of my life, my only true purpose is to protect other women from great harm with the gift I have been given.

So this book is for you, to help you understand and spot those monsters who seek to consume your light until you are nothing but skin and bone, your soul enslaved to their control, your existence defined by their mood. Your life left in a tailspin and them still hunting you, maliciously seeking to kick you while you are down. Trying to force your own hand to end your life.

I am almost 49. I fled the country to escape him. Now I live in my best friend's house and try not to think of the beautiful home I had, the car I loved to drive, or the garden I nurtured. The few scraps I owned from before the marriage are stored in a shipping container, locked away for who knows how long. Perhaps forever. My narcissist was incredibly successful in his work.

He has all and I have ... nothing.

Except this. My words.

And those can never be taken from me.

So let us begin.

This time with the truth.

PART I | THE HUNTED

SANCTUARY

It's late. Everything is closed and it's dark. In the industrial orange glow of a solitary street lamp, I wait at the back of an empty mini-bus, its interior aglow in garish pink and blue neon lighting. I'm the last of the passengers to leave and am glad to escape its condensation-soaked interior.

There is a strong scent of wood burning in the heavy air. I inhale, grateful to cleanse my lungs of the ripe odour of unwashed humans. The air tastes of silence, and long, dark nights and quiet, unchanging days. Of a place locked outside of the passage of time.

A two and half hour flight from London. Five hours on a train, then another hour and forty minutes crammed into a sweaty mini bus stopping and starting its way towards Slovakia and the mountains of southern Poland.

Cocooned in a muggy drizzle of foggy air I eye the deserted bus terminus. It's very small. My bags hit the ground with a loud smack and my attention lurches back to reality. The mini bus driver gives me a dirty look loaded with Polish condemnation. I want to apologise for the weight of them but I don't know how. No one speaks English here. No one.

He slams the rear doors closed. It sounds resentful.

Without a word, he leaves me under that ugly orange street lamp, gets into the empty bus and drives off in a thick cloud of dirty exhaust. The handful of others who were on the bus have already departed for their fireplaces and hot showers. I am alone. It's very dark. Panic touches my spine.

What the fuck have you done?

I don't answer. Because I know it's not my voice. It's *his*. And I know if I answer, it will only get worse for me. It always does. He always wins. Even in my head.

Even now.

One year exactly after the day our divorce was finalised, it's still not over.

That's why I came here, to a place where I would be vulnerable, alone, and safer than I have been for a very, very long time.

I came here to heal, to write this book. But right now I am freaking out. Old triggers are lighting up inside me like fireflies, threatening to set me aflame in terror. I can hear his voice rising, mocking me, derisive, calling me a stupid cunt, and a selfish asshole for doing a stunt like this in the middle of a pandemic, saying I deserve to be tricked and left alone in the dark. That he hopes I die here in the gutter of Poland where I belong. I close my eyes to shut out the noise of him, to concentrate, like when you turn down the music when you're driving to focus on where you are going.

Just breathe. He will come. You are OK. You are not a stupid cunt. You are brave. You are courageous. It's not a gutter.

Footsteps approach. I turn, my heart pounding, fear eating me alive. A man pulls his medical mask down so I can see his face then he lifts up his phone and in its white glow I see my Airbnb profile photo.

Darek.

The brother of the woman who owns the flat is there to collect me as promised. I don't bother to hide my relief. I smile. Giddy. Elated. Safe. Safe. Safe. I practically run to get away from that street lamp, from the bad words that were inside me. But they follow me, as they always do.

But not for much longer, because I have a plan to end the tyranny of the toxicity my once-husband buried within me.

I have learned that in silence, there is doubt, and where there is doubt there is control. Words will liberate me from the lies. The pain. The sorrow. The hopelessness.

Words will become my weapons in this silent battle to restore my life to myself, and this fight is not only for me but for every woman who is enduring, about to endure, or is in the aftermath of her endurance in one of the most hellish scenarios imaginable.

Let us begin together then, the work of unpicking the lies, one by one, and with these words we can heal our wounds, and give ourselves our power, our hope, and our lives back.

To do so, we must go back to the beginning. To *their* beginning. It starts in infancy. Narcissists are made, not born.

In the normal development of an infant, it is assumed infants do not perceive any separation between themselves and their caregiver. They cry, get a response, and calm returns. This cycle of trust paves the way for the eventual understanding their caregiver is separate from them, and the infant is able to develop an awareness of separation, of the 'otherness' necessary for the development of a healthy ego. This is the crucial point where the foundation for the healthy give and take in adult relationships is laid.

It is when this fundamental assumption is fractured via neglect, carelessness, absence, or abuse, that a narcissist is made. Denied the opportunity to understand their caregiver is a separate being from them, the cycle of trust never begins. The door to the development of a sense of 'otherness' necessary for healthy relationships remains not only closed, but vanishes altogether.

All they know is a void. An emptiness. They cannot trust their needs will be met. This is a place of terror and misery. A place of enormous uncertainty and fear, far too overwhelming for an infant to process in any possible way.

The damage is permanent. No medicine can help. No therapy will mitigate the damage they will cause to themselves or to others from their inability to understand they are separate from others. They must live for the rest of their lives nursing the deepest of wounds, which cannot be healed.

Psychologists call this fracture 'the narcissistic injury' and narcissists are doomed to live with it for the rest of their lives, unaware of its existence, or of the immense harm it causes them to do to others. Or, of how they unrelentingly see themselves as a victim no matter how deep the cruelties they dispense upon those who've had the misfortune to orbit into their world.

No amount of love, care, or compassion can heal them. They are destined to live with the outgrowth of this breach in their development for the rest of their lives, where it will only fester, fed by an unending cycle of negative feedback loops they will manifest through destructive behaviour and relationships, over and over again.

This fracture is the root of narcissism, and NPD (Narcissistic Personality Disorder).

It is a tragedy to think this could happen to an innocent baby, and as an empath, I find it heartbreaking someone could have such an awful destiny bestowed on them.

But any time we begin to feel sorry for them, we need to remember this: they are unaware of their injury and never will be. Their blindness is perhaps a mercy. It is a construct created in infancy to wall themselves away from the magnitude of their fracture. They do not see their suffering as we see their suffering—their loneliness, their anger, their blaming, their constant search for fulfilment and never finding it. They are incapable of it. You can try to explain it to them, but you will only be met with derision, or worse, you will be accused of making them that way.

But, this book is *not* about them. It is about *you*, and what you can do if you have been caught in the snare of narcissist, or are being targeted by one.

The great American author Joan Didion said when she doesn't know how to deal with something, she learns everything she can about it to give her power over it. And so, let us take a leaf from her book and learn about the ones who were doomed in infancy to live in emptiness, incapable of love, empathy, compassion, or personal responsibility—unable to understand we exist separately from them and are not things which are an extension of their world whose only purpose is to enforce or validate their skewed perception of reality.

It is said the only way to protect yourself from a narcissist is to go no contact.

Easier said than done, since they are masterful at getting what they want, and when distancing oneself from a narcissist, one must be extremely careful because they are capable of unimaginable vengeance if you leave before they are ready (since it triggers their original injury). I had to flee the country, and even now, one year after our divorce he still hunts me through the courts seeking to make me pay him for having had the misfortune of having been his wife.

As terrible as it sounds, the 'safest' way to get away from a narcissist is to be discarded by them, but by then you will be a shell of yourself, barely alive, your light consumed by them from their endless dramas, fights, accusations, demands, abuse, and gaslighting. Your mind, body, and soul will be in its weakest position to face the aftermath that will inevitably follow if there are children or a divorce to be faced. No, it is hardly a 'safe' exit. But it is the unfortunate lesser of two evils.

Narcissists are drawn to empaths like moths to a flame, only, this breed of moth has evolved with flame-proof armour designed to extinguish the beautiful fire of love and light that burns within us. They settle over our trusting light, their black-armoured wings beautiful, complex, and enchanting, with us unaware it is a dance they have repeated over and over and left countless others in the ruined, broken shadows of their lost light.

It is comparable to addiction, their ingrained need to feed on others to fill the void within them, of their inability to see others as separate beings with feelings, needs, wants, and desires of their own. No, we exist only to nourish them in a sick cycle of insatiable emotional, and psychological vampirism. We are not individuals to them. We are nothing more than a supply that exists for them to fill the endless void that seeks to consume them. And when they have drained us of our last scrap of energy, they look at us with derision and leave without so much as a backward look (the discard), to begin the cycle all over again with a fresh, bright new target brimming with supply (whom they have often already begun to seduce with their victim narrative while still in a relationship with you).

For a time, while our light is burning its brightest, they place us on a pedestal, and tell us we are wonderful, perfect, the best thing that has ever happened to them. We believe it because they are convincing liars, or perhaps because they know it is exactly what we want to hear, and we long to believe it. It doesn't matter. It works. You have what they want, and they will stop at nothing to get it, like a junkie desperate for their next fix, they will lie, cheat, steal, and deceive until they can take from you what they do not have themselves.

Manipulation is their strongest skill, and without any moral compass, you are destined to be putty in their hands. And the deeper and greater your empathy, the stronger your appeal, the bigger the seduction . . . and the harder you fall.

THE FALL

I am walking on air. I cannot believe my luck. I have just met the perfect man. When my best friend gave me a copy of *The Secret* to read I was doubtful that airy-fairy crap could ever work, but in the year that has passed since my broken engagement to a Danish guitarist I felt I had nothing to lose. I began to visualise exactly the kind of man I wanted to end up with: Sensible, mature, smart. Good job. Nice looking. Good with his hands. Manly. Interested in me.

I still can't wrap my head around the concept that visualising the kind of man I wanted to meet would actually turn up, and so fast. But he did, and he's exactly the one I have been waiting for my whole life.

He did stare at your breasts a lot more than your face.

I brush away the unquiet thought. It's true. He did look at my breasts a lot. It made me a little uncomfortable. At one point I even reminded him I was 'up here'. He didn't seem ashamed or embarrassed though. Just smiled in a cocky way that reeked of confidence, like he already knew I was going to be his.

He was so interested in me, wanted to know all about me, and he listened carefully, asking questions in a way that flattered me, and encouraged me until my throat grew so raw from talking I had to stop. I realised far too late I knew hardly anything about him and he had the advantage of me. What was it he said when I pointed this out? 'You are far more interesting than me.' Then, before I could say anything more, he left to buy me another latte exactly the way I like it.

It began at Copenhagen airport. I felt his eyes on me, watching me in a way that said: 'You are going to be mine'. It wasn't love at first sight, but damn, the electricity that snapped through my body from that look of his, of being watched by a man as beautiful as him, of having been selected out from all the others . . . I was both intimidated and flattered all at once. He had the advantage right from the start.

He asked if he could buy me a coffee. I said yes. We spent four hours in Starbucks. He was so male, so big and strong, he made me nervous but in a delicious way. He had beautiful hands. I couldn't stop looking at him, at how perfect he was. I couldn't believe he was real. Handsome, tall, clean cut, smart, witty, an engineer, travelling for work. Masters educated, fit. The ultimate alpha male. Perfect. Perfect. Perfect. Just as I had visualised.

We agreed to meet again when he returned from Germany at the end of the week. I would pick him up from the airport and he would stay at my flat before he continued his onward journey into Sweden on Sunday. He kissed me goodbye, a chaste thing but with the promise there would be more.

Much more. I shivered with delight. Perhaps it *was* moving a little too fast, but it just *felt* so right. Anyway, who was I to question destiny?

We spoke several times during the week and on Friday evening I went to get him, my gut screaming I was making a huge mistake. I listened to it, uneasy, because usually my gut was good with its instincts, but no matter how I combed through the conversations I'd had with him or his behaviour (apart from the breast staring) I couldn't pinpoint why my gut was panicking like a wild thing trapped in a cage, so I turned the music up and drove faster towards the one I knew was meant to be my soul mate and told myself it must only be nerves.

We eat the roast I cooked. We drink single malts. We kiss. I tell him I want to wait to sleep together since things were moving so fast. We fall asleep on top of the bed, still dressed and full of whisky.

I wake sometime in the night, my jeans around my knees and him riding me.

'You are inside me.' I am so stunned, I can only state the blindingly obvious.

He says yes and continues doing what he is doing.

'But I was asleep.' Also obvious.

He smiles and kisses me.

Nothing like this has ever happened to me before. I am locked in disbelief. He is so calm. It makes no sense. Is this rape? I don't know.

'Please. Stop. Get off me.'

He slows and looks down at me, the room too dark for me to see his eyes. 'But you started it,' he says with what sounds like genuine confusion.

I push him away from me and sit up. He sits back onto his haunches. He is naked, unlike me. I haul my jeans and underpants back up and notice I am wet. How could I be wet? Nothing makes sense. I pinch myself hoping it's just a bad dream. It's not.

'How could I have started this?' I demand, starting to freak out. I have no idea how to handle this. I glance at the clock. 3 am. I had been asleep for 4 hours. The last thing I remember is falling asleep, the taste of whisky in my mouth. 'When I have been asleep until now?!'

'Not as far as it has been for me,' he says, and I see him shake his head. 'It was you who started it, you turned to me and started to kiss me, you woke *me* up. I thought you were awake. You were moaning the whole time.'

I blink. Stunned. He sounds so sincere. I don't know what to think. I can't think. Everything feels weird and wrong. I have never ever had anything like this happen to me before.

I open my mouth to tell him I think it's time for him to leave when he says, quiet: 'I am not a rapist. I swear I thought you were awake. But I can tell you don't believe me. I'll go.'

Guilt slams into me. It's the way he says it. Like I have hurt him thinking he could do such a thing.

Shit.

He slides off the bed and bends over to pick up his jeans from the floor. Unhappiness surrounds him. I let him dress. I need time to think. At the door he turns back to look at me.

'What will you do?' I ask.

'Drive home,' he says.

'It's a five hour drive,' I say. More guilt. I *was* wet. If he had been forcing me I would have been dry, right? Maybe he is telling the truth. I don't know. I don't know what to do.

He says goodbye, low, and turns to leave.

I crack.

'Wait.' I whisper. 'Stay. We'll figure this out tomorrow.'

He comes back and lays down beside me, his clothes still on. I say nothing, and neither does he.

He falls asleep before me. My gut churns. I wonder if this was the warning it had tried to give me. Uneasy, I watch him sleep. Then it begins. I rake over the evidence, the possibility he could do such a thing to me. I had been very attracted to him the night before, maybe I did start to kiss him while half asleep and didn't remember. I had drunk a lot of whisky after all. Maybe I hurt him making him feel like a rapist. He has only ever been a gentleman with me. I decide he is telling the truth. I fall asleep and never bring it up again.

When you're caught in the grip of a narcissistic relationship, the one thing you are absolutely guaranteed not to have is clarity. Or certainty. Or peace.

Your world will be one of constant instability, with brief lapses of false stability that end for no reason at all. When you ask a question to gain clarity, or attempt to understand the cause of a bad atmosphere through open communication, you slide down a rabbit hole of accusations, caught in a confusing cycle of blame that has nothing to do with the conversation at hand. When it is done, the situation is far worse than it was at the start and instead of just one question needing clarification, you now have twenty.

You retreat. Hurt by their words, accusations, and refusal to come to a place of understanding and peace, your thoughts spin like windmills in a storm, your emotions drowning in an ocean of confusion. You cry. You feel sick. The one person who could bring clarity to all these uncertainties is the very one causing them. The feeling of betrayal is enormous. The feeling of being controlled, suffocating. There is no balance, no peace, only chaos in your mind, body and soul.

And then the silent treatment begins, so there is zero hope of getting any clarity in the next hours to days. You have no choice but to sift through the turmoil of what you just experienced and try to make sense of it alone.

But there is no sense to it. Because it isn't about open communication, understanding, and compromise. No, it's about control, power, and a need to draw on (even feed on) the emotional energy you expend navigating each of these fabricated-out-of-thin-air crises.

Once you are done crying and you drift, exhausted, into an all-too-familiar numb reprieve, your beautiful, good, kind, innate sense of empathy kicks back in, and you find yourself trying to see their point of view, since your own no longer makes sense. You reason they must see something you can't.

They were so forceful in their views, perhaps, as they said over and over, you didn't listen properly. Or maybe you really are that stupid. Or was it dense this time? No, thick. You are thick.

And then, your thoughts swerve in a direction your gut hates, maybe they *are* right. Maybe it *is* all your fault. Maybe you started it all. Maybe you are the problem.

But that's the thing. You don't know exactly what the problem is.

If you take just one thing from this book, it needs to be this: It's them.

The problem is *them*.

But right now, and for a long time, you won't understand this, because when you are with a narcissist, you are groomed into a mindset similar to Stockholm Syndrome. You know your partner is not treating you right, but to survive you make excuses for them and blame yourself, and the very thing that made you powerful—your empathy—is turned into a weapon and used against you.

And this is going to be your greatest challenge, to understand what has been stolen from you, and to reclaim your empathy and give it back to yourself, instead of pouring it into their endless void. To love yourself back to life again.

It's the evening before the beginning of the Easter weekend. I haven't seen my husband for almost two weeks while he has been staying at his flat five hour's drive to the north and working on a consulting job. I have ordered a bottle of expensive single malt whisky for him from me and another, less expensive one from the cats. He had complained earlier he didn't have enough single malts in his collection, though at my last count I found 20 bottles. But some were almost empty and I guess it's important to a man like him to have a lot of choice, so I used half my monthly allowance he gave me to buy him two bottles of whisky and then planned lots of nice things for the weekend. Good food, wine, and of course chocolate treats for Easter Sunday, even a little plan to hide chocolates around the house for him to find.

I am giddy with expectation. I know this is going to be a good weekend. For once we will have a good time, nothing will go wrong. I have made sure of it.

I give him a quick call just before I go out to get all the shopping and collect his Easter gifts, and to see if he wants beer.

He answers, and I say, bright and cheery, 'Oh you are still at work!' It was only 3.30pm, but I had half feared he was already on his way and I would run out of time to prepare all I wanted to prepare and cook dinner before he arrived after working on my writing all day.

He says yes he is, but he will leave soon though. I say, oh no hurry I still have lots to do and then ask about the beer, since the liquor store will be closed for most of the weekend. No. He doesn't want beer. He sounds the tiniest bit annoyed. I cannot imagine how it could be anything I have done, it must be something at work stressing him out. I ring off with a wish for him to have a good drive and set off, happy and excited to gather everything together in preparation to shower him with my long-planned surprises.

It's dark and the street is wet with rain as I come out of the liquor store with the bottles of whisky and my bank account depleted. I don't care, I know it will make him happy—even the person who handed me my delivery said it was a gorgeous malt and that I had good taste. I am so happy. Everything is coming together perfectly. He will see I am a good wife, how much I love him and cherish him and care for him, because he has said I don't and I need him to see how wrong he is. I know everything is going to be amazing. This time there will be no mistakes. This time everything will be perfect.

My phone rings. It is him. I drop my bags into the passenger seat and get into the car, answering as I go.

'Hi!' I say breathless with the walk and my hurry to answer the phone and not keep him waiting because he hates that. 'How is it going?' I ask, meaning his trip.

'Not good,' he says. I note the tension in his voice.

'Oh?' I ask, as light as I can not wanting to worsen his mood, 'Is the traffic bad?'

'No.'

Silence. Ominous. Heavy.

I wait, uneasiness creeping up my spine. I wonder why he has called if he isn't going to say anything. Something is definitely off, and I sense I am the transgressor. I rake through everything that has happened between us over the last days. Nothing. Nothing. Nothing. I have been perfect. I haven't given him anything to complain about. I hear his windshield wipers against the windshield of his car squeak. He shuts them off in stony silence.

Dread claws at me. I sink back into the driver's seat knowing this is it, the beginning of the next cycle of whatever it is I have done wrong. The silence drags on so long I cannot bear it anymore so I ask: 'Are you OK?'

'No,' he says, so terse the word comes out like granite. It slams into me and I feel my ebullience fade. Here it comes. I brace myself. I know this drill. I hate this drill.

'You have totally ruined the weekend,' he begins, his tone scathing, liquid hate. 'I don't even know why I'm bothering to come down to see you.'

I wait, my mouth dry with fear. I have no idea what I have done, but from his clipped words I know it's serious, he's furious and getting angrier by the second. Stupid, stupid, stupid me. Frantic, I try to think what I have missed, of what I did wrong to earn his wrath.

I can think of nothing. Blankness washes over me, fills me with terror. Please. Let me be wrong.

'Is the traffic bad?' I venture, timid, into his wrathful silence.

'No.'

'Something happen with your parents?' Hope slashes through me, he has been known to have altercations with his father. Maybe that's it. Maybe I am overreacting and everything will be fine. I just have to ask the right question.

He laughs, cold, harsh. I hear the windshield wipers switch back on and eviscerate the abyss of silence growing between us.

'You wish,' he says, dark. The atmosphere thickens. I sense the metaphorical crack of his knuckles, his anticipation.

I blink, taken aback. I don't know what he means, but I guess at his meaning. I wish it was about them, because it's about me. My heart sinks to my toes, through the floor of the car and onto the rain-slicked road. I brace myself for it. Like the roils of nausea, it's reaching its crescendo. It will come soon. The purge. And my heart will burn in bile.

I feel tears cutting into my eyes, the constriction in my throat. Terror stalks me. This one is going to be bad. I can feel it in my bones. I glance at the bags containing a fortune's worth of rare whisky in the footwell of the passenger seat. My gifts to him, the hours I spent researching to find him the perfect bottle, the order I made two weeks in advance, how I had to save my allowance for two months to pay for it. My gaze drifts to the sweets I bought from the bakery to surprise him in the morning. I feel cold. The rain starts to fall again. I watch it slide down the windshield, my soul locked in misery.

He starts then. It doesn't stop for a long time. I have the phone on speaker and have to turn it off because he is yelling so much people walking by look into the car, taken aback. There are a lot of swear words. Mean words. Hurting words.

Stupid cunt. Worthless waste of space. Piece of shit. I wish you were dead.

His fury rains down on me punctuated by savage presses on his horn to force the cars ahead of him out of his way.

At last, panting with rage, he tells me my crime. It was when I said: 'Oh you are still at work!'

I am told I ruined his day. He was fine until I called him and criticised him for being at work and not already on his way down.

Relief floods me. Because it's not true. Not even close. It's just a misunderstanding. I called to find out whether he wanted me to buy beer at the liquor store, not to check where he was and if he was on his way. I never asked him anything like that. I know that for sure. I definitely, purposefully did not ask that question because I know it makes him mad. I can't understand why he is saying I did when I *know* I didn't. He must know I didn't. I can fix this. Hope surges.

'But I didn't criticise you,' I begin. 'I—'

I want to say it was because I was *pleased* he was still at work, because it meant I had more time to prepare for the evening because I had overspent my time writing. I want to explain everything, of how I still had a lot to do to prepare, to make sure everything would be ready for him when he gets home but I don't get a chance.

'DON'T DENY MY REALITY!'

The thunder of his wrath stuns me. Passers-by look into the car even though I am listening through the handset. I huddle deeper into my seat, drowning in humiliation and shame. My hands start shaking. My body follows. Fear snakes through me as I realise how little time I have to prepare myself for what I will have to face. I know him too well. When he gets like this it can take days for the silence and retributions to end. I am afraid. So afraid. He will be home for five days. It's unbearable. I can't think. I don't know what to do. I want to run away, but

I have nowhere to go. He has everything, all the money, all the power, everything. He owns me.

He is still screaming at me, incoherent with rage. I hear the engine of his car accelerating hard as he speeds down the motorway in the pouring rain. I am afraid he will get into an accident and it will be all my fault. I am desperate to make it stop, but it's like standing in front of a mile high tsunami and hoping your body is enough to end it. The hate pours over me. Everything is my fault. The traffic is my fault because he was angry after the call, so he was late packing up and leaving. The rain is my fault. The stupid woman driver he just passed would not have been there in his way if I had of just behaved myself. Now he's stuck behind another shitty, stupid woman driver. He could have just stayed up north, but no, instead he is coming to down to see ungrateful, horrible, shitty, shitty me.

He goes on and on, until he runs out of immediate things to say and begins the next stage, when he rakes through the past, of the multitude of other times I denied his reality. I listen, numb, as he cycles through past events, changing facts and omitting truths so his narrative becomes one streamlined soliloquy of hate and victimhood.

I know better than to say anything—to try to steer him back to the truth, to what actually happened during those events, of witnesses who also saw what happened, who have confirmed the truth of things, to defend myself from his accusations—because if I do, he will latch onto my words, twist them around and use them as fuel to hurt me more. No. I am wiser now. Silence is my only defence.

I want to hang up but I am afraid what will happen to me when he gets home if I do. He has made it clear I am not allowed to hang up. Ever. No matter what. His words are important and I am not to disrespect him by cutting him off.

I have no choice but to endure the onslaught, to wait for him to run out of steam. His words hit me like weapons, until I am drenched in lies, half-truths, and a campaign against my Self that becomes so convincing I begin to think maybe he is right. I wonder if I am really that stupid, that I cannot see things right, and he is the victim and I am a bad, ungrateful wife. I feel worse than shitty. I feel terrible. I want to die. I am a horrible person. The man I love is furious with me. I did it wrong. Again. I didn't do things right. And I was so careful not to do it wrong.

Rain hits the windshield, forms into sinuous rivers in the orange glare of the street lamp. My face is wet. I don't remember crying. I wonder if the rain is coming through the windshield and hitting me too. He cuts the call off mid-vent. His last words are, 'Fuck you, you fucking—'

Silence slams into me. The drum of the rain against my little red Aygo fills the void. I am lost. Adrift. Fear paralyses me. I am shaking. It's cold. I start the car, blast the heat and stare out the window for a long time, watching the rain, my mind crawling into itself, making itself small, invisible, like I want to be. The familiar feeling of shock settles around me. I welcome it. One hour ago I was happy and filled with hope. Now I can't comprehend what's happened. I sift through the wreckage of words, try to piece it together. He decided I did something, got angry and now I am in trouble. When I tried to tell him how it was for me, tried to communicate, I denied his reality. There is no way forward. Only his narrative. And now I am going to be punished.

For something I didn't do.

Or did I?

Other couples walk by with carrier bags full of wine, beer, and groceries, readying for the long holiday weekend. I wonder if they will go to the cinema and eat popcorn at some point. I would have liked that. Now I know that won't happen. Nothing will happen but fear. One of the couples are holding hands and talking to each other. My heart aches. It's all I want. That. Just peace. Love. Nice times. But I do everything wrong. He's right. It's all my fault. I ruined everything. It's easier to blame myself than to fight him. I have to fix myself. I need to pay better attention. If only I hadn't said those words, how different this evening would be.

It takes a long time, but eventually I pull myself together, drive home, unpack the shopping, wrap his gifts and begin to cook his dinner, one of his favourites that takes two hours to make. Uneasy with apprehension, I wander around the house while the dinner bakes in the oven and saturates the house with delicious smells.

I tweak the towels in the bathroom so they are perfectly square. Light some candles around our beautiful, expensive house to make it cosy, or perhaps to stave off the emptiness clawing at me, to banish the depth of the lie my life has become. I don't really know anymore.

I pause to touch up my make-up so the last of the evidence of my tears are erased, though I cannot hide my unhappiness, the downward slant of my mouth, the sorrow of my soul. I try to smile. No. Better not to. The fear in my eyes makes me look strange. Unhinged.

I drift, aimless, my heart tight with dread, alert to the sound of every car that passes outside, checking and rechecking to make sure everything is perfect, tidy, clean, the table laid for dinner, the wine uncorked, everything precise, so there are less things for him to complain about, less things that might make him angry.

But there is always something. Always. I know I will never think of everything, because I am stupid, and I make stupid mistakes. That I don't deserve him. That I am lucky to be with him. That he could get rid of me and no one else would love me. There is only him. I know these things are true because he told me this many times over the past six years. Without him I would die, he would make sure I am left with nothing, he promised me that. I would be old and unwanted and poverty-stricken. And he would take all. It keeps me awake at night. This promise of the ultimate punishment for having displeased him. I would rather die than face such a life.

Therefore, I cannot imagine living without him, of running away to a woman's shelter and leaving my cats behind where he might hurt them or abandon them out of revenge—I do not even dare entertain the thought of escape, for fear he sees it in my eyes and tightens my bonds even more—nor can I imagine living without this fear, without his control, without the punishments, beratings, deprivations. Without the violence.

Even though I hate it, I don't know how to make it stop, nor do I know how to live without the legacy of this pain, this uncertainty. I have become lost in the thrall of his power as he feeds off my suffering and misery, of his brutal control over me, over whether I survive, live, or die. I don't know how to make it stop, all I can do is try to do things right, and not make him mad. It's survival. That's all. And I am terrible at it. I catch a glimpse of my hollow expression in the hall mirror, and wonder how long it takes to die of a broken heart.

They say some people make you feel like you are walking on eggshells around them. Yes. Only mine are made of the finest glass, and when they break, they slice me open and I bleed, my happiness, hope, and love trailing behind me, a silent testament of my life's destruction. He takes it all. Everything. He owns me. I will never escape.

He eats the dinner in silence, hunched on one arm over his plate, shoving the food into his mouth as if it is a punishment he must endure. He picks up his wine and drinks while looking aside, as though I am offensive to look at. Even the way he swallows his food and wine resonates with the seethe of his anger. It flares off him, tangible, whips me, hurts me, frightens me. I try not to let him see my terror since that also makes him mad. I take tiny bites of my food, my stomach in knots, sick with unease. I make sure to eat quietly, to make myself as small as possible. I don't speak. I don't dare. I keep my eyes down and only cut quick, furtive glances up to check his progress through his meal. He finishes and puts his cutlery down, precise, perfunctory.

I put my cutlery down too, even though I am in the midst of cutting my food. I cannot eat when he is not eating, I feel too vulnerable. I never know what he will do next when he is like this. I swallow the food in my mouth and wait, tense, alert. Scared. I notice the cats have not come to greet him. I can't see them anywhere. They didn't even come out when the dinner was served to ask for a titbit of meat. They know. They are hiding. I hope they stay hidden. I am always afraid they will get hurt when he flies into a rage.

He hasn't said a word to me since he walked in. Instead, he has ignored me, or rather behaved as if I exist but as if I am nothing more than an object, or a piece of furniture, walking around me, blanking me. I get up and clear the table, desperate to get away from him, from the radiance of his hatred and resentment.

While I am at the sink, I hear him rise. I hold still. Brace myself. He leaves the room, grabs his bags and heads downstairs to the master bedroom, his heavy footfalls ricochet through the house, purposeful, reminding me of his size, weight, and strength. Of how quickly he can break me. I know its meaningful. He doesn't always walk like that. Only when he wants to make a point.

I get the point. I note the warning. I wonder where I am supposed to sleep tonight. Does he want me to sleep in the bed with him, or should I go to the guest room? I let out a trembling breath and start to rinse the dishes to put them in the dishwasher, seeking to soothe the jagged edges in my soul with the gentle actions of domesticity. I feel something brush against my leg. I jump, my nerves fired for flight.

A quiet meow rises, a timid question. My youngest cat, Nova, looks up at me, fearful, her eyes huge in her head, seeking reassurance. I realise she has been in the kitchen, hiding under the island the whole time. Guilt slams into me, as it always does when it gets like this. The cats are living in fear, too. And they have to watch the one they love get hurt, over and over, cornered by another's powerful body and screamed at, his face right up against their mommy's and the litanies endless; watch her shoved into doors, walls, stairs; choked backwards over furniture until she can't breathe anymore; thrown to the floor. Fractured bones. Tears. Pain. Blood. Bruises. But it's the words that are the worst. Screamed at the top of his lungs, as she is told in withering detail of her worthlessness, her uselessness, her unattractiveness. Her unlovableness.

I should be protecting my little ones, instead, it's this. Russian Roulette day in and out. I gather her up. She climbs into my arms, clings to me, her claws digging into my arm and shoulder, her head tucked into the curve of my neck. I hear her purr, but it's not a happy purr, its the kind of purr cats do when they are scared and try to soothe themselves. I stroke her, whisper reassurances, tell her it will be OK, but we both know it's a lie.

It won't be OK. It will only get worse. It always does.

I know what I have to do.

I finish clearing up the kitchen. Start the dishwasher and turn off the lights. Nova returns to her hiding place. The other two are nowhere to be found.

I go downstairs to the master bedroom. He has taken his toiletry and laundry bags out but hasn't unpacked the rest of his bag. It's sitting by the door, his polo shirts and jeans neatly folded inside. I know what this means. It's a threat. *I can leave any time and then you will be alone on Easter weekend, and everyone will notice I left you alone because you are shit. How humiliating that will be for you.*

He is on the bed, looking at his phone, utterly ignoring me. I walk deeper into the room, and stop in the middle, out of striking distance. I wait.

'Yes?' he asks, cold, his eyes on his phone as he continues to read whatever it is he is reading.

I note his posture. He's in his underwear, sitting propped against the pillows, his muscular legs crossed at the ankles. The muscles in his arms bulge just from holding his phone. He takes working out seriously. It shows. I swallow, my mouth dry.

'I'm sorry,' I whisper.

He keeps looking at his phone, though he stills the tiniest fraction. I have his attention. He says nothing. I know he's waiting for me to continue, to add more. I don't let him down. I need to survive. I need peace. I need to protect my cats.

'You are right, I was wrong.' I say, hating the trembling of my words, my throat constricting on the lie I must speak to avoid worse pain.

He sets his phone onto the bed, deliberate, like an annoyed parent being disturbed by a difficult child and folds his arms over his chest. I get a cold look shot at me, the first one since he walked back into the house an hour before. He waits, his glare on me, expectant, demanding.

'I made you feel pressured about coming home, and I am very sorry I did that to you and ruined your day.' I don't try to explain my side. There is no point. There is only one way forward. To confirm his skewed narrative and annihilate reality, the alternative is too painful.

'And?' he presses, vindication sliding over him. I watch him relish it. Savour it.

I expect this. I know how he is. I know what he wants. What he needs. And I give it to him. Because there is no other choice. I think of Nova's big eyes. Her fearful purring. I compose myself and kneel. Bow my head and eviscerate my soul.

'I don't deserve you, thank you for coming home. I promise to be better.' The words come out. Not my words, the words of another. Of the one trapped and trying to stop worse to come. I hate who I have to be, but I need her.

'Wash your face and come to bed,' he says, terse. 'You look like shit.'

And that's it. I rise. My head still bowed as though in the presence of a tyrant king and leave. I wash my face. Check the doors are locked. Find Nova and reassure her mommy has fixed things for now. She stays in her spot, which leaves me uneasy.

I return to the bedroom. It's dark. He is laying on his side with his back to me. I don't think he's asleep, but I am grateful for this reprieve. Nothing more will be said.

I dare not turn the light on. I slip into the bed, as far from him as possible. I am cold, the sheets are cold. I stare at the slice of light shining in from the hall, a diagonal slash of white across the ceiling and wait to sleep.

It takes a long time. And when I do, I dream of love. Of another who cherishes me. Who cares for me. Who caresses me and kisses me, who tells me I am beautiful, who looks at me with love. I dream of the one I must live for, of the one my soul longs for in the midst of its chains. I wake. It's four am. I get up and go to the bathroom and lay down on the floor. It's warm in there. I take a bath towel and lay it over me, a makeshift blanket, and think of the one I dreamed of. No one I know, but he made me feel safe, a rare thing, I had forgotten what that felt like. Nova comes in and lays down beside me. I pet her soft fur. She purrs. A contented purr this time. My eyes close. This time I dream of nothing.

It isn't always bad. That's what makes things so complex, what made me fall deeper into his reality, and distance myself from mine. Because when it is good, it is incredible. A fairytale. Perfect. He is the dream husband. I feel like the luckiest woman alive.

During those halcyon days I begin to wonder if I remembered the bad times wrong, if maybe I had somehow made things worse than they were with my 'over-active imagination' as he called it. He said I fabricated things in my head, remembered things wrong.

And during these good times, I doubt myself. Doubt my memories. Because when things are good, it feels wrong to remember the bad things—they seem unreal, far away, impossible even. Imagine you are standing outside in a heatwave in the middle of July and you are so hot you feel like you are melting and then try to imagine that same spot in the winter, knee deep in snow locked in subzero temperatures, your fingers numb with cold.

You can't. It's like that. Up and down. Heatwave. Snowstorm. Heatwave. Snowstorm. No spring. No fall. Nothing in between. Two extremes. It goes on and on until the trees melt and the sky implodes.

And him, beside you, reminding you day in and out you remember everything wrong.

You shrink into yourself. Huddle from the chaos. Endure the horrible times. Crave the good times. Don't think. Don't question. No. Definitely don't think. It's too dangerous.

It's easier just to let him decide everything, to have all the control. Let him tell you how it is, even if it is the polar opposite of what you see, hear, experience, and feel. To survive, you need to annihilate your Self. But in this place of annihilation, at least it's peaceful. Safer.

And you want to be safe. You want the house and furniture to be safe, not smashed up in a rage. You want the cats to be calm and relaxed, not vomiting up their dinner and shitting liquid diarrhoea after he goes on a rampage and scares them sick.

But the price you pay for those rare days of ephemeral 'safety' is steep.

More than you can even imagine.

I know. Because I am still paying the price more than a year after it ended and the divorce has been finalised. He continues to hunt me, fabricating claims against me and taking them to court, wasting its time and my meagre amount of money on the lawyer I need to protect me from utter ruin. My ex knows what he's doing. He has the money, the income, the power, the connections. He won't stop until he breaks me. Bankrupts me. He was always very smart. Calculated. Dangerous. Vindictive. It never stops.

On July 25, 2020 as my SAS flight prepares to depart from Arlanda, Stockholm, I open my text messages to write my first communication to him since his birthday four months earlier.

Like all things, he has controlled everything, has even prevented me from having closure. He simply ignored me while continuing to assault me through his lawyer, his father, and the court, using them to do his dirty, dirty work for him.

At times during the year after he left me for another woman, he would turn up in his car and just sit in the driver's seat for 15-20 minutes in his sunglasses and stare at the house, saturated with hate. It was terrifying. I would huddle under the window ledge and listen for the slam of his car door, the heavy tread of his footfalls on the path, my fingertips on the panic alarm and positioned in range of the security camera so if I hit the button, it would trigger the camera to record everything. To see everything. To allow others to watch me die. Living with fear like that is tangible. Visceral. Brutal. It changes you.

I dared not call the police. I was told by the authorities he has the right to come to the house, since he owned it and has the keys to it. I was not allowed to change the locks unless the court gave me right of access. I could only call the police if he hurt me. Staring at the house he owned was not hurting me. They made that clear. What did they know? It hurt. It terrorized me.

Worse still was the knowledge the police were far away. It would take at least forty minutes for them to get to me even at the quickest response. My social worker had explained everything to me. Only call when you are in danger. But that's a fantasy, as any woman who has endured the horror of interpersonal violence knows. When you are being thrown around like a doll and crashing into walls and slamming into furniture, stalked by an enraged man with the veins in his head so swollen you are afraid they will explode, how do you make a call to the police? How? You can't. You just can't. It's impossible. When you are in a situation like that, it's all about making it end as fast as possible. You are scared out of your mind. You are in pain. There is blood. There are fractures. There are bruises and welts. You are panicking. You try to escape and they block you, like a cat tormenting a mouse. You wonder if this time you will hit your head on something and die. When it's really bad you actually hope you will, because then it would be over.

Fear. Always fear. And vigilance. Day and night it continues long after he is gone. I claw myself free of nightmares of him stabbing me, cutting me, hitting me, cornering me and screaming at me, his hands clamped around my throat until everything goes black, or, the ones I hate the most, when I believe I have woken up and he is there in the dark, watching me, the smell of his cologne washing over me. I would wake up screaming, already reaching for the panic alarm hidden under my pillow.

But he was not there. It was the memory of his hate he had buried in me. It lived on. Unending. His legacy. A phantasm in my soul. Something my mind could not escape. It still has not escaped. Not even with the medication for C-PTSD I take every single day. I still dream of him. I still wake up screaming.

After what would feel an eternity, my leg muscles cramping and my heart pounding, I would hear the crunch of gravel and the rev of his engine. I would ease myself up, trembling like a leaf in a storm and watch him drive away, a rush of cold sweat my only warning of the retching to come. My soul ragged with fear, I would empty my guts terrified he would come back while I am still vulnerable and puking.

During the year after he left I never felt safe. I was afraid all the time in those months after he discarded me, as he sent others to torment me, to gather information from me, to have them threaten to deprive me of any financial support if I didn't sign the papers they'd prepared that would defraud me of all my legal rights in the division of assets, and to turn what few friends and supporters I had made against me. And to always,

always remind me I was totally dependant on him and he called all the shots.

No. I never forgot that. Not once.

I stare at the empty text field on the screen of my phone. I am a writer. Words are all I have. My strength, my shelter, my sorrow. So I wrote my longed-awaited message of farewell, granted my heart the closure he denied me and spilt tears of relief as I pressed Send.

It had been hell to get out of Sweden in the middle of a pandemic. COVID-19 left lockdowns all across the planet. Flights were grounded. Borders slammed shut. I needed to be out of the house by the end of May regardless of the world grinding to a halt or I was made aware my situation would go from worse to very, very bad.

And he and his parents did not disappoint me. They took my car on a slim legal technicality, leaving me stranded in the middle of nowhere with a sick cat that needed veterinary care. I rented a car. It cost a fortune. I tried to be brave, but the truth was I cried all the time. I was scared what would come next. I feared the electricity would be cut off, or the Internet. I waited, anxious. A fish turning round and round in a barrel, waiting for the inevitable shot. Longing for it.

I wanted out, more than anyone could imagine. I was able to secure a place at the women's shelter, but then I learned I could only take one cat with me, and the other two would have to go into foster care for at an indeterminate period of time— perhaps forever. I couldn't bear it. I clung to the hope the ban would drop in the summer and I would get out of the country with my three cats. Somehow.

But I couldn't get out. Nor despite going to extreme lengths could I find another legal rental because I didn't have enough income from my writing. I couldn't even order an Internet connection in my name. Deep into May 2020 no flights were allowed to land in the UK from any Scandinavian country. I know because I tried to buy a flight out from every country.

All I could do was wait for the ban in the UK to lift. And no one knew how long that would take. Meanwhile, the campaign of hatred against me increased, the threats deepened. I lived in terror. Thoughts of suicide stalked me night and day.

A heavy thump washes into the cabin's hush followed by the thick grind of the door's interior mechanism locking. The plane is sealed for flight. At last. For the first time in thirteen months it feels safe to breathe. I exhale through my medical mask. Relief shreds me. Tears scorch my eyes.

I had made it. I had escaped him and his parents and survived their campaign of bullying, threats, terror, and tyranny despite everything they had done to isolate me, break me, disempower me, and leave me destitute and homeless.

Except I was wrong. I might have fled the country and put a sea between me and him. But I had not made it. I had not escaped. And this is the hard part. The part that is difficult to accept, harder to write, but critical to expose.

No one warned me. Not one person prepared me for what would come next. I had watched all the YouTube videos from other survivors, from the best therapists, psychiatrists and psychologists on narcissistic abuse, saved important articles in a secret Tumblr account, and read the books. I thought I knew what I was doing, and what to expect. The advice was clear. Get out and go no contact. Everything will be OK. You will heal. He will forget about you and find supply elsewhere.

It was not OK. Not even close. Perhaps it was because the woman he left me for did not want him after all, and he took his vengeance out on me or, maybe my narcissist is exceptionally controlling and couldn't accept the one he had imprisoned for almost a decade had escaped his multitude of traps.

Or maybe, as I began to suspect, these survivors, specialists, and therapists on YouTube didn't reveal the full truth of what can happen when you get out and go no contact with a narcissist because they feared if they did, those of us trying to leave would lose our courage and not go. Perhaps. I know it might have made me hesitate. But still. I would rather have known than be caught unawares. Not knowing is worse. So much worse.

It's a cruel thing to give people hope and lead them to believe if they just do *x* then *y* is guaranteed to follow. And *x* is not easy to begin with, it takes every scrap of your strength and energy to make that disconnection when your mind has been remade in your abuser's narrative, when every action you take to protect yourself is diametrically opposed to your programming.

You are riddled with doubt, fear, anxiety, and the sickening, terrifying feeling of severing the deepest of trauma bonds, so thoroughly embedded into your identity, it has become who you are. Worse, as you try to disconnect, you discover you perversely crave their control, their abuse. Need it. You are lost. You fight yourself, your poisoned thoughts, and learned patterns, circling round an endless cycle of locked doors, and the only one open to you is the return to pain. You resist, a solitary creature in a dark hell, alone, lost, adrift.

No one understands this kind of isolation, this kind of pain. No one. Because those who do are also isolated, alone, and silenced, caught in their own labyrinths filled with dead ends. Lost between the spaces of life. Ghosts. Shadows. Seeking to live, but instead, slowly dying from the inside out.

You are told if you just break the connection, escape, run away, go to a shelter, to a friend, to family, and stop all contact you will get better. No. It doesn't work like that. This is a half-truth. Not a whole truth.

No one warned me about this. So I am going to warn you.

If you are in a narcissistic relationship and you have found the courage to begin to plan your exit strategy, know that your journey back to yourself, to the freedom you once had, of having your own thoughts, your own choices, your own opinions, of living your life on your own terms is not going to be easy—No. You will be in for the fight of your life on two fronts. I'll explain.

In a normal break up, you decide it's over, pack up your things, and leave. There will be moments of regret, sorrow, pain, perhaps even brief and stormy reconciliations. But ultimately, it's over. It ends. It just. . . . dies. You move on. You forget. You live again. Love again. You might even become friends again. Maybe even go to each other's weddings years later. That's relatable. Movies are made about it. People get it.

Not this. On the first front, even if you have been discarded, even if you go no contact, even if you move to another country—they are still there. A constant presence. A threat. A nightmare. They pursue you through the courts with their expensive lawyers, lies, false evidence, and constant claims of victimhood when it is nothing more than a vendetta with one solitary purpose—to remind you they still control your life and can annihilate you, the vice-grip of their fist on your leash, unrelenting, laden with the heavy reminder of the utter dominance, power and tyranny they had over you and still have over your life, your existence. That they will never let you go. Why would they? They need the supply you give them. The drama, the sense of victimhood they cherish (and will tell with disturbing conviction to anyone who will listen).

On the second front is your trauma bond. The deep fracture which has split the foundation of your Self into two, that chasm that has separated you from who you are and left you in a desolate place where you must be who they tell you to be to survive the unending cycle of abuse, punishment, reprieve, reward, inconsistent rules, rewritten history, gaslighting, judgement, abuse, punishment and so on until your reality is completely subsumed by the narcissist's and you become nothing more than an extension of their chaotic version of reality.

This is the part no one talks about. There are not enough flights in the world to run away from the brutal legacy of your trauma bond. Even if you could run away to a colony on Mars, it would not be enough. You can't escape what's buried inside you. I know. I tried. I ran to the UK. It didn't help. Now I am in Poland writing this. And he has followed me here, a spectre of hate and vengeance, insatiable for my destruction. The court case continues. Two precious days of healing, and of writing were lost in the return to the past, in reliving the horror of being stuck in his world, of having to do whatever it takes to stop him from hurting me more, of going over all the pages of claims, fabrications, and false narratives backed by emails he had cut and paste together to make it look like what he wrote, I wrote, of fighting against the lies, the misrepresentations and falsified documents submitted to the court. It does not stop. Day and night it goes on. Not safe. Not safe. Not safe. It never stops. He will never stop. The nightmares do not stop.

And yet, despite the hell, I cherished a quiet, private, romantic hope, that perhaps the affection of another could begin the cascade of healing the trauma within me, that to feel loved might awaken the dying part of me I had lost, breathe life back into my soul. Now I know the truth. After more than a year and half of not being touched by a man, another has held and kissed me, his skin against mine, a man I adore as a friend, his tender caresses the last mark left on me instead of the one who only hurt me—yet still it does not stop. The trauma. Still. For those precious hours the pain inside me dissolved, I felt happy, free. But when we drifted to sleep hand in hand I knew no one could love me out of this place of brokenness. Only me. And I didn't know how to do it. Another hope died that night at 3am. It was OK. I was used to it. But still. How to end this pattern? How to find peace? How to heal? For months I had cherished this hope. Nurtured it. Tended it. And now I must let it go.

I stand alone, on the fracture line of my Self where I remain trapped, and gaze at the remains of the woman I once was languishing on the opposite side of the abyss, lost without me. How shall I reach her? How shall I return? Not like this. Not from the touch of another, no matter how true, how good, how beautiful. It is not enough. Love is not enough. At least not the love of another.

The next morning as he slept, I sat cross-legged on the bed in the wan morning light, showered, empty, hollow and sad, and faced the black and white headboard, bleak, thinking perhaps I would never escape, as thoughts of ending my life returned, and beckoned to me, offering the peace I desperately longed for.

He woke and asked me if I was OK. I told him the truth, because we are close like that. He fought it, of course. Argued passionately against it, raged against the unfairness of my being the one to die when the one who has perpetrated such crimes against me continues to go on, thriving, wealthy, and able to continue hurting me until I break. He knows he cannot help me. He cannot save me from myself. He can only offer the reprieve of tenderness, support, and friendship, but nothing more. I never asked him to give me anything more. I don't want him to. I want to save myself. That's why I am writing this. For you, to help you, and maybe to help me, too. Although it is costing me much more than I expected it would. But that is something I will return to later, not now. I am not ready to write about that part, yet.

DARK, DARKER, DARKEST TIMES

You'll hide it. If you are in relationship with a narcissist right now, or are trying to figure out how to get out of one, you will know exactly what I am talking about. You have been made into your own worst enemy—have trained yourself to believe what is happening, isn't.

Deep inside, you internalise their awful narrative, that you are the problem—the cause of the stress, drama, their rage, and take all the blame, expect it. Even if it decimates you, you accept everything is your fault and no matter what you do, you will still be wrong—because there have been far too many painful consequences when you attempted to communicate, to be heard, to be understood. To matter. No. You have learned it is better this way. But still, neither can you live with the burden of such a terrible reality, one where there is no hope of you having any power to make things better without beginning to fragment into pieces.

So, you blinker your mind from the pain and focus on those rare times when things are good. And those times *are* good. So good. You feel *grateful* for them because they are so good. You might even post about your perfect partner who loves you so much they whisked you away on a luxury weekend break and treated you like a queen. You share the photos of your suite in the centre of Stockholm at the most expensive hotel, of the wine, food, intimate meals, the room service breakfast, how he poured your tea and arranged your plate with the best things to eat. The lovely things you saw wandering around the city. How happy you were.

It's a dream. You cling to it. Build it up. You make him a king. You want him to never stop being that man. You think if you enshrine it in digital pixels somehow all the bad will magically go away and the good times will stay.

You do this. Create rules. Dozens of them. Little deals you make with no one but your imagination, but somehow, it helps you cope, gives you a sense of control of the uncontrollable. If this, then that. 'If I write lots of nice things on social media praising him, he will be nice to me. I will be safe.'

Of course, it never works.

But you cannot help yourself. You create a false narrative. You believe it. You need to believe it. Because it hurts far less to live in self-deception than to accept the truth: That you are hated, and you will continue to be hated and hurt until you find a way to escape (which once you are backed into a corner and utterly dependant on them is extremely difficult) or you die. And at times, you do hope you will die. At times, you hope the next time they throw you around the house you will hit your head and it is the fatal blow. That you will never get up again.

Of course, it never happens.

Then again, you don't even know what's real anymore. *Everything* is a lie, the past a constantly shifting, changing thing dependant on his mood . . . so why not create your own lie, a beautiful one?

Deep in the broken part of yourself, on the other side of your fracture, the real you, the one you lost knows you are hiding the ugliness of your life from other people, that the existence you project of being a happy homemaker with a great, successful husband who dotes on you is an utter lie—and you are the biggest perpetrator of the propaganda.

These thoughts tend to be strongest in the dead of the night, when you wake and stare at the strip of white light shining across the ceiling and silence saturates the house and the truth escapes its bonds for a heartbeat and slides through you. Defies your lies, your constructs. Wills you to see what he has made you into and asks you to fight back. Begs you.

You sit up. Listen. Everything is clear. So clear. Yes.

And like a cruel plot twist, he wakes. He sits up filled with care and concern and puts his arm around you, asks if you have had a nightmare and to lay down beside him where he will protect you.

The truth slips back into its tomb and buries itself alive as you obey and lay down beside the one you can neither hate, or defend yourself from. You let him tell you everything will be OK, that he will take care of you as difficult as you are, because if he doesn't, no one else will.

Then he sleeps.

And you weep.

When the abuse begins again, as it always does, out of nowhere, that fresh hell where he comes after you, enraged for god knows what, as he shouts at you, and cycles through his litany of hate, eviscerates your character, shreds your shared memories of the past into a new narrative that blindsides your sanity, you race to do damage control, desperate to get the cats outside to safety where they hide wide-eyed under the deck chairs, and close the windows so neighbours and passers-by won't hear. So the cats won't hear.

It's how your mind works in trauma. It doesn't make sense to those who have not experienced it. But I am not writing this for those people. I am writing this for those others who are locked, right now, in the same situation, so you know you are not alone. What you are living through, day and night, I lived through. Each and every grim, soul decimating moment. I understand every facet of your anguish, your sorrow, your pain, your isolation, your hopelessness. I was there. In many ways, I still am.

I will not mince words. You are in for the fight of your life. But right now, I am here. I will stand with you and fight with you, by your side. I am not strong, but I have my words. They are all I have, but they are yours. If they help just one woman to survive the lies, the accusations, the brainwashing, so she gathers the strength not only to escape, but to survive, to heal, it will be worth the anguish it has caused me to write this, to relive this.

The pattern is always the same. Like the steady drip of a broken tap, little by little you become isolated, physically, emotionally, mentally, financially, your dependence on them, utter. And with each drop that strikes your essence, your boundaries, your protections, your hopes, your identity, what makes you, you, fades and becomes another, a simulacrum you don't recognise. By your own actions, you commit the crime of shrinking your world into nothing because you are led to believe it will bring the peace and harmony you long for, because you want the awful accusations to end, the toxicity, the negativity, the bad atmosphere to go away. You think if you just concede to this one thing, they will be happy. But they are not. Drip. You concede to another thing. Drip. Another thing. Drip. Another. Your world evaporates to the bare minimum. Tea. Feed the cats. Clean the house. Water the garden. Cook. Write stories. Wait for him. Wait on him. It is incredible how effective this method of chipping away at someone's foundation destroys one's sense of self, certainty, and trust in what's real . . . and to make what is not real, real.

You agree to cut contact with your support system because he doesn't think they care about you, that you can't trust them. He plants deep doubts in your mind. You fight those doubts for as long as your strength and will holds, contacting them in secret, but he can tell when you are getting stronger, when you resist his abuse, when you dare to question his rewritten version of the past that makes you the monster and he the innocent victim. Things get worse. The accusations against your family and friends deepen, become more sinister, conspiratorial. Paranoia creeps in. You start to wonder if he can see something you can't. You feel stupid. He tells you they are jealous because you are well off and they want you to break up with him so you won't have what they don't. You become unsure. He is convincing. He takes you out for dinner. It's nice. He seems to really care. He holds your hand as you walk back to the car, opens the car door for you like a gentleman. Treats you like a precious doll. That night he takes out the lavender oil he bought for your birthday and rubs your arms with it until you get sleepy. He kisses your forehead and leaves. You drift to sleep feeling safe. Protected.

Doubts plague you. He is there, caring for you. They are not. You speak to your support system less and less. You bask in the glow of your husband's approval until . . . there is only him.

When the shit finally hits the fan, you are caught off guard. You're not fast enough to react, but you try anyway. You close the doors and windows to silence the violence of his hate, and position yourself in range of the door, primed to run, wishing to god you had your shoes on but you don't.

How many times did I run out of that house in my bare feet? I don't know. Too many. I never realised I hurt myself until much later when I found the cuts and scrapes in the soles of my feet, the gravel buried in my blood.

As he storms through the house, and screams in your face about how worthless you are, and how you have ruined his life, his voice as powerful as an army commander in the heat of battle, you fear the closed windows are doors are not enough to contain his fury, that the neighbours will call the police.

You beg him to stop yelling because you are afraid the neighbours will hear, that the police might come. He bellows: 'Fuck the neighbours.'

You cringe and hope the windows and doors are enough to hold in the vitriol. That people can't hear what's happening to you. Things would get complicated. You would be asked questions you can't face answering. It would break the fragile narrative you have so carefully built to make it all stay glued together until you can figure out a way to escape. No. Better just to endure. You know what you are doing. You know how this goes. You know you will cry. Your mind will twist and turn for days sickened by the poison he is burying into your mind, the pain in your heart will consume your nights—but neither are you ready to face the world alone, broken, weak, disconnected from yourself, the prime focus of his hate as he seeks to fulfil his promise to eradicate your existence into extreme poverty.

So, in those moments where he is not attacking you, when he is not bending reality with his narrative, or creating tension so thick in the house you begin to suffocate, you hide the bad times from yourself. This dissonance is the only way to make sense of the senseless. To organise the chaos of each day into their ugly, jagged lines, their edges sharp, waiting to catch you up, to slice you into smaller and smaller pieces until only the memory of you is left. A memory that is a lie.

You make yourself small. You wear bland clothes. You stop wearing make-up. You have very little control left in your life.

You can still make tea. You cook, but there is no joy in it because he doesn't speak to you as he eats. You have the cats. You cling to them, to their companionship, their presence, riddled with guilt because you don't know how to save yourself let alone protect them.

In your darkest moments you think of putting them to sleep and then killing yourself. Safer that way. To escape through death so the hurt will end, forever. You image their little bodies lined up on the floor, their light gone as you lay down beside them, close your eyes and fly away, free. All of you. Together. Safe at last.

Those were dark times. Very dark times.

DISCARD

On the longest day of the year, he left me while I was in the shower for the woman I later learned he had been seeing for over a year. It was my fault. Of course.

She had a boyfriend. But the phone made it easy for them to stay in touch when he wasn't in the north in the same town as she—at the same gym as she frequented.

My god how he protected his phone, he carried it with him everywhere, locked tight as a drum—I know because when he was in a hurry to get into his phone, it took him ages to get through all the passwords, thumbprints and codes. He said it was for security for his job. But he is just a consultant electrical engineer, not Jason Bourne.

I suspected it was because of me he made all this effort to lock his phone because he had something to hide. But he gave me far too much credit. I was so naïve I didn't even know what WhatsApp was, let alone how to crack a phone's security.

One fine spring morning, I go into the kitchen to make tea. He is in the dining room with his back to me, engrossed in his phone, scrolling through messages and photos. It has a green theme. There are a lot of photos, though I can't make them out. I had never seen such a platform before. I am only allowed to use text messages. I know nothing about apps or how to post pictures on my phone. I'm not allowed to lock my phone and I know he goes into it, because things would disappear. Once, the entire history of our texts vanished. I asked him if my phone would have done that. He said yes, because I used too much data. Much later, I learned the truth. He had done it. Why? Because there were horrible texts in there from him so he deleted history. He was good at that.

I didn't like what I was seeing. I didn't want to see it. I pick up the kettle and pop its lid to let him know I am there. In the dark glass reflection of the extraction fan I see him switch his screen off and hit my back with one of his withering looks. He asks if I was spying on him. I say no, I only just walked in. He asks what I had seen. I say just some green stuff, that I didn't have my glasses on so it was blurry anyway. I act as if I have zero interest in the matter. I hope I am convincing.

He says it is his work messenger. I accept his lie without question. I don't say I think it is strange there were so many photos. Why would I want to do that? Although it doesn't matter. Already I am gravitating towards his words, to the comfort of his denied reality. It is true. It is for his work. It is just his colleagues sharing photos of their weekend adventures. It's a social feed for his job. Yes. That's it. I cling to that because it feels better than facing the alternative. That he's a total liar who is sitting at the designer dining room table I paid for and hitting on another woman.

I go to the sink and turn on the water. He watches me, narrow, suspicious, like he doesn't believe me—like I am the one who is the liar and not he. I wish I hadn't come in to make tea. I offer to make him a coffee, to change the subject. But it is too late. He sets his phone down, deliberate, like he always does when he is building up to what he does best, where he convinces me I am the monster and he the victim. He might as well take off his shirt, fold it carefully and set it aside. The message is clear.

'I am coming to get you.'

No. Please no. I avert my eyes, make myself small, submissive, hoping it will pacify him. I fill the kettle, try to keep my hands from shaking.

He rises from his seat and prowls up the steps into the kitchen and positions himself over me, blocking me, cornering me, his presence dominating, threatening. I can smell the coffee on his breath. It stinks of bitterness. I am still holding the kettle. I clutch it to my chest, the water inside sloshing back and forth; put it between me and him and wedge myself into the corner of the counter, my head down.

His voice gets colder, harsher, sharper. Louder. He accuses me of being paranoid, of giving him no peace, of always making him have to answer for things he shouldn't have to answer for. It goes on for a long time. I don't look at him. His words hit me like rocks, they hurt. He calls me names, those familiar cruel words that pour from the mouth of the man I love and never get used to. I cringe, but say nothing. When he finally stops, panting, his hands clenched into fists, and his eyes daggers of pointed hate. I whisper: 'I am sorry. You are right. I make your life hard. I don't deserve you.'

There are tears in my eyes. Of fear, of remorse, of shame. I don't disagree with him. I believe his litanies. That he suffers to be with me, that everything is my fault, that I make him miserable, that he wishes I would die. That his life would be so much better without me in it. I don't fight it. I tell myself I remembered it all wrong. I did come in on purpose to check on him—like he said—and not because I was in the midst of my writing and craved a fresh cup of tea for having written a scene I was proud of. No. He's right. I remembered it wrong, because I am a liar, even to myself. That's how monsters are. They lie so much they can't see what they are. I am a monster. I deserve this. I deserve nothing.

He doesn't stop. He drives his point home, long after it has already pinioned me to an abyss of hopelessness and despair. It's relentless. My knees give out and I slide to the floor, still clinging to that damned kettle. I weep, broken, hating myself, wanting to die for the awful creature I am. I ask him if he wants me to kill myself, to make things better. I mean it. It's the only gift I have left to offer him. My life. I want to make it better. I want to make it stop. I could cut my wrists. Get into the bath. I am numb with grief. I can't bear my existence. I am ready to die. To end it. To make him happy. The last good thing I could do to prove I love him.

He laughs. I blink, stunned. I wasn't being funny. Fear slices through me. Rides rough over my despair. The narrative is changing, fast. I know this one. The switch. I glance up at him and even through the haze of my tears I can see it in his eyes. The vindication, the pleasure. The sadism. I can't keep up.

He tells me this is the problem. That I am crazy. That he is stuck with a crazy person. Only a crazy person would react like that.

He repeats my offer to end my life in a mocking tone. He laughs again, in cold contempt of my anguish, of my desire to right the terrible wrong he has placed on me.

I don't know what to do. To say. So I say nothing. My body tingles with terror, anticipating worse. But he is done. He is satisfied. He leaves me and returns to his seat at the dining table, picks up his phone and unlocks it. Ignores me. His posture dares me to so much as look at him. I suspect he is back on the screen with the green theme, looking at the photos of someone else. It hurts.

I gather myself together. Stand. My nerves jangle, firing for flight, but I hold myself still. I put the kettle on the hob and switch on the heat, prepare my tea cup, the milk, and wait for the water to boil. In the extraction fan's black glass, I glimpse my tear-stained face. Humiliation claws through me. I can't even begin to piece together what has happened, so I don't. I came in to make tea. So I make tea and go back to my desk, wipe away my tears, bury the last thirty minutes of my life into the grave of all the other hurts, and continue to write.

He had left me once before, for a couple of days, four months before the day he left for good, in late February. It was just one month after we had moved house, when the lamps and blinds were still waiting to be hung and the house was infested with silverfish and the heating didn't work properly. He tried to fix it, but said it was impossible, he would have to think about what to do next. Of course it didn't bother him because he barely lived there, he was spending more and more time in his flat in the north. I remember being cold all the time. Even in bed under a pile of blankets.

The cats would come to me at night, their noses as cold as ice. I would tuck them under the blankets with me and we would huddle together, shivering, miserable. Those nights were long. Unhappy.

I remember that February day clearly. It was a Thursday. He was working from home, but by 10.30am he was already gone. I know this because I videoed him from the bedroom window as he drove away in his 5 series BMW. I marked the date and time in my calendar. I don't know why I did those things, but when you are numb you are reduced to the menial. To record keeping, as if it somehow matters.

That time, he went into a rage over something I hadn't done, a construction he crafted from out of the air, another misunderstanding like so many others similar to the one I endured that brutal Easter weekend. It was pointless to defend myself, because then I was denying his reality, so I conceded, I apologised for something that didn't exist, anything to get the peace back. I even got on my knees and begged. I was afraid. I didn't want him to leave. The heating still didn't work. There were silverfish in the beds. I didn't want to be alone in a cold house that wasn't familiar without blinds, without lights, seething with creeping, slimy things. He had promised he would fix those things, would make the calls I couldn't because I wasn't allowed to deal with it, he had to control everything. But he refused to hear anything I said. I was judged, condemned, berated, and shoved aside, a thing in his way. He was leaving and fuck me if I didn't like it. I deserved to be left in a cold, insect-infested house.

His rage escalated faster than usual, even for him. I wondered if this time he would kill me. The violence he rained on the house, the walls, doors, furniture was terrifying, filled with the promise of what he would do to me if I got in his way again. When he started punching the island in the kitchen, I spirited myself away and hid under my bed. When I slid myself underneath, I discovered my three cats already huddled there together deep in its recess, their eyes wide, focused on the entrance to the bedroom, defensive, scared. Like me.

I slid up to them, and gathered them to me, my little babies. They clung to me as he rampaged through the house, packed his bags, punched more walls and stormed up and down the stairs, screaming his hatred at me, of how much he wished I was dead. I held back the tears of fear. Of terror. Of the silence of my existence. Of guilt. Welcomed the calm of shock, sought the presence of mind to think what to do if he found me, how I would protect the cats. Protect myself. He searched closets, throwing them closed so hard I expected to find them broken afterwards, demanding to know where the fuck I was. I held my breath and waited for him to go. Willed him not to figure out I could hide in such an obvious place.

He gave up, eventually.

The front door slammed. In the driveway, the thump of his car door closing, followed by the throaty roar of his engine surging to life. I hauled myself out from under the bed in time to video his departure. That way I knew it was real. He was gone. It was over. I was alone. And it was my fault.

It was a party. He caused all that to justify leaving me so he could go to a party in the north that night. To see *her*.

I discovered the truth much, much later, but it didn't help to put things right inside me. By then, it was far too late. The damage was done. Because after he left—after I marked the time of his departure in my calendar, and a particularly large silverfish used its tiny feelers to explore the floor near my feet—I absorbed the hate he had poured into me. Internalised it. Blamed myself for the terrible atmosphere he had left behind. I was bad, I was worthless. How could anyone make anger like that up? Only someone thoroughly awful could cause such a reaction in another human being. I was too dense to see how horrible I was. I deserved to be left. He was right. No one would ever love me. Ever.

I think I cried. But I don't remember.

The day he left me for good, I didn't see it coming. It was June 21, Midsommar Day, Sweden's national holiday to celebrate of the longest day of the year.

Every Swede celebrates Midsommar one way or another. With friends, drink, food, parties, town-wide festivals, dancing around a flower-strewn pole, or just getting quietly smashed at home. The next day the country falls into utter silence as an entire nation nurses the worst hangover ever. It's surreal. I love the day after Midsommar. The silence. The peace, the emptiness. The feeling as if I were the only person alive wandering in a wild, remote place. It felt apocalyptic. It was great to be a writer on that day. To experience that.

The morning of Midsommar Day, I get up early to write. I am in the midst of writing the final book in my series. At one point I need to calculate how long it would take Thoth to run a certain distance at a certain speed so the timing in the narrative would be realistic. I hear my husband go into the kitchen. He has been in a good mood so far that morning. I decide to chance asking him for his help.

I go in to make tea, ask if he would mind helping me figure it out the math since he knows a lot about both math and running. He is pleased to help and when it is a good day, like today, he likes it when I consult him on the more technical aspects of my work. Plus he is smart, and gives good, useful answers.

I loved him for that. Admired him.

As I boil the kettle, brew the tea, and make him a coffee he helps me wrap my head around how I can make the pieces fit. We talk a little further about what else I intend to write the rest of that morning before getting ready to celebrate Midsommar with his parents. I leave with my tea, pleased by how things are between us and continue writing. I feel good. Everything is going well between me and him. We are having a nice day. He is being nice. He even smiled a few times. I love his smile. Especially when it is bestowed on me.

When I hit my writing target, I ask if he wants to join me on my daily walk along the canal, something I do to clear my mind each day from the intensity of writing.

He says yes, but the darkening of his mood in the three hours since we spoke is tangible. I rake over the last conversation we had. Nothing. I had been good. I had been grateful, and let him know how much I admired him for his intelligence. Since then I had worked, and it hadn't taken longer than I promised; I hadn't made him wait. I can think of nothing I have done, nothing I could say or do to put the brakes on wherever this is heading.

Then it occurs I must have said something he has had time to dwell on, to twist into something else. I catch the look in his eye, the one I dread. I *have* done something, but as usual, I will not know what it is until he tells me. It will be something he has built into something else, fabricated from the dark corridors of his mind—something I won't be able to defend myself against because if I do I am denying his reality. You can't argue with that.

I should have gone on the walk alone. But I am afraid to leave him with whatever is brewing in his mind. If I go alone, it might make him more angry with me, and I don't know what I will come back to. I dare not ask what is wrong because he will deny there is a problem, even though the atmosphere is drenched in his mood, of the promise worse is to come.

Once again I face a hated, familiar crossroads. Two options rise on the horizon, both guaranteed to lead to more hurt, more suffering. The goal is always to choose the path that leads to the least hurt, only in his case, all roads lead to hell. Always.

I always thought I had some control over that choice, but now, as I write this, I see I did not. It was a construct I created to give myself a sense of power over my fate. It was a lie, like everything else I told myself to make sense of the impossible. He always had all the control.

I taste the suffering to come, my destroyed appetite, the acid scald of fear, dread, powerlessness, of not knowing what will come next, the collar of his dominance wrapped around my neck so tight I cannot breathe. Of there being no escape.

After almost a decade with him, I know the steps to this dance very well. He will become enraged by whatever crime he believes I have committed against him. There would be no trial, only his accusation delivered in a haze of fury, my judgement and the punishment.

Next comes the indeterminate period of banishment as a human, of being ignored, deprived of money or necessities, or abandoned in a parking lot miles from home with no money or any way to get back, or perhaps for a lesser crime, of what minimal privileges or promises he has granted, stripped away, or—most terrifying of all—of him leaving for his flat in the north for days on end, erasing my existence, refusing to answer my texts, or emails, refusing to give me my allowance so I am penniless, and me going on, wondering, waiting, anxious, his poisoned words feeding on my mind, condemning me—without any idea when he would return, or if he would ever return.

Those were the days I wanted to die the most. The days I knew I was nothing to him. No one.

Then, once my despair reached its deepest, when I was ready to do anything to make it stop, the steps of the dance change, abrupt, like a savage, cruel tango. He would come back to me, find me in his car as I wandered, weeping and lost trying to make sense of my abandonment; or come into the office and offer to make me tea, or ask to watch something on Netflix together, offer a cuddle on the sofa. He would pour me a glass of wine and act as if none of what had happened, had happened, and I would be so grateful I would go along with it, pretend what I had just lived through, the long horrible, terrifying hours and days of uncertainty and fear a mere figment of my overactive imagination.

So, like a homeless kitten starved for love, I let him cuddle me, as my heart sought to mend in silence the anguish he had driven into it, to convince myself it hadn't been as bad as I remembered. Or if I could not do that, I settle on the fact I must have deserved what he had done to me. But now I was forgiven, and that was all that mattered.

When he gave me those reprieves I clung to them like a woman released from the horror of solitary confinement, desperate never to be sent back. I believe so long as I behave myself the way he wants, I can stop it from happening again. I always swore in those moments to do whatever he wanted, no matter how humiliating, no matter how much it denied what my senses told me otherwise. But I always fucked up. Always. I know, because he said so. In detail. I didn't remember it the same, but he was so certain, he had to be right, and I wrong. I didn't know what was real anymore. It was too hard to fight it. Better to just accept it. I never was right anyway.

By the time he left me, my mere existence was enough to drive him into a rage, into violence. I would be condemned and thrown back struggling, pleading, weeping, and terrified into my cell of silence and powerlessness—while he, the possessor of the keys to my long imprisonment would secure the lock and walk away. Sometimes he smiled, cold, cruel, satisfied.

The pleasure he took in my suffering as he locked me into my hell, as he revelled in his absolute power over my existence tore me to shreds. Those times something primal in me reared up. It wanted to kill him. To make it end. To end him. In those moments I wanted him dead. I could taste it. It never lasted. I am not a killer. I am not him. No. As he left me locked in the silence of my punishment, it was easier to blame myself. To let him decide all. Even whether I lived or died.

I don't want to make it real, acknowledge his mood on that Midsommar Day, or ask him what is wrong, because the reason would certainly point to me, as it always, always did. I had to choose: continue as I had begun and endure the wait for him to reveal my crime or walk alone and return to him and find him even angrier for having left and walked without him . . . or worse, find him gone again for another indeterminate length of time. And no knowledge of what I had done this time.

Fear hijacks me. I choose to continue as I had begun, hoping it will be the lesser evil, that the walk will lighten his mood. I smile and say it is a beautiful day and put on my shoes.

Bathed in sunshine, we walk under a cerulean, achingly perfect summer sky, the wheat in the fields verdant with gold-furred fronds. He is silent. Resentful. His ugly mood a blot against the beauty of the day. A barricade, laced with aggression locks me outside of him, an impenetrable fortress to which I walk round and round in search of an opening, a crack where I might gain admission, find forgiveness, and be spared the isolation of his hate. My heart tight, I cling to the fading remnants of our earlier conversation and continue to chat, as bright as I am able to, about what I had written after we had spoken—of how grateful I was for his help.

He doesn't look at me. The distance between us yawns, intentional, a deafening message. I quail. Whatever I have done, it is serious. My thoughts career ahead, into the woods, past the fields, up into the skies, searching, like the hawks circling above, seeking sustenance

I console myself with one thought: we would meet his parents in a few hours. If only I could hold out until then, perhaps this will pass. He will drink and eat tonight and he might feel better towards me after.

He was brilliant at hiding his dark moods from others, could switch from being a monster to a perfect, doting husband in the blink of an eye. It was terrifying to witness. And yet, I, ever the desperate fool would go along with it, thinking it was over, that things were better, and bask in his loving attention. My god, sometimes he would even feed me something from his plate in front of them, as if he adored me, and others would smile, indulgent and pleased for our blissful union, but always, as soon as we were alone, the mask would fall and the hate would begin again, worse than ever.

I keep talking, nervous, about the flowers, and the butterflies. About the birds. About all the flowers that have been taken from one part of the meadow for the Midsommar tree and how sad it makes me for the bees and the butterflies to lose so much just so people could celebrate a pagan holiday. I try not to babble, but I do. I say things I know he likes to hear. His silence becomes stonier. He clenches his fists and walks faster. I have to trot to keep up with his long strides.

Perched once more on the knife-edge of his mood, that precarious, terrifying place between peace and annihilation where he is the sole master, I hope I can make it stop with my words. I try to make it stop with my words. My useless, pointless, wasted words.

He orders me to be silent.

His tone ensures I shut up. Regret feeds on me. I made the wrong choice to walk with him. I have only made whatever he was angry about, worse. We walk on, him ahead of me, and me trying to keep up, like a subservient squaw. I am invisible to him. In my haste to stay apace with him I trip on a rock in the path. He doesn't look back. Humiliation slays me. Dread slides into me, a shadow.

Eventually, we return to the house. I am sick with anxiety. I must bite my lip not to ask what is wrong. I dare not ask. I know what happens when I ask. Bad things. Please not today, of all days. Let this not be a bad day. It's Midsommar, the whole of Sweden is celebrating, is happy. I want to be happy, too.

He lays down on the kitchen floor on his back, his knees bent, and says he is tired. I leap for this olive branch. Say I understand, that he does so much work and must drive so much for his job that it is no wonder he is tired. That it is good he has the long weekend off to rest and relax. I am so careful with my words, make sure to say nothing that will cause offence, only show my support.

I am on one of the bar stools at the island, ridiculously grateful he is talking to me, lying down and not standing up and in my space where unpleasant things can happen. I nurture a faint hope his mood has passed, that the walk helped after all. That maybe everything will be ok.

He gives me a filthy look.

He is on his feet. His fists clench, a threat, a promise. The yelling begins. He pushes himself into my space so fast I am startled from my seat. Panic grips me. I try to slide away from the corner he is shoving me into. I fail. He pins me in the narrow space between the jutting corner of the wall and the solid weight of his chest. The corner's edge digs into my spine. I concentrate on that. On what that feels like. It's important. It's real. The rest is not. It's a bad dream. A lie. What man could do this to a woman he loves?

His face looms over me, his eyes bore into mine, hard as granite. Remorseless. His mouth moves, almost touching my lips, but instead of a kiss, of love, hate pours out. Vitriol. Words I know by heart. The ones I hear in my head even when he is not there, that I have indoctrinated into my soul, embedded into my heart, and worn into rutted paths in my mind. I want to close my eyes but I am held hostage to his hate, to what will be next. My worth is decimated. My existence willed to silence. It goes on and on. But there is nothing new. Just the same things, recycled. It still hurts. He can still hurt me.

He leans back to catch his breath, to gather new words to hurl at me. That primal thing inside me roars to life, reacts, and I slip, like quicksilver out from under his arm and dart across the kitchen. Out of reach.

He turns, paces towards me. Fury slams into me and I welcome its embrace. I rise. Enraged. Ready to fight to the death. At last.

Fuck you. I scream. Fuck you. No more. I won't live like this anymore. This ends now.

And then it evaporates. My courage. My strength. I run and lock myself into the bathroom. I expect him to kick in the door, to break my neck. To finish me. I have never defied him like this before. I don't know what comes next. I have driven the pattern so far from of its course anything can happen. I look for something to defend myself with. There is nothing.

I sit. Trembling. No. Quaking. Terrified of myself. Of the magnitude of the rage that enveloped me as I turned on him. As I snarled back, showed my teeth for the first time in my life. How I was ready to die, was ready to fight to the death. My death. Perhaps he saw it in my eyes.

Because he does not come.

I wait. And wait. He storms around the house. Banging. Crashing. But he never comes to me. I wonder if this was all I ever needed to do. Stand up to him. His rage continues to rain on the house. But still. I am left alone.

I calm. Organise my thoughts. The pattern will return, I think. What will come next will be my punishment.

Numb, I resign myself to my fate and get into the shower. I don't know what else to do. I don't want to come out of the bathroom. As the minutes tick past, well worn behaviours, old friends born out of the habit of survival tell me what to do. Keep up appearances. Bury the pain. We must go to his parents for dinner soon. Get ready.

I take my time in the shower. Try not to think of the consequences I will inevitably face. As I switch off the water, the sound of suitcases hits the floor of the hall. It's intentional. He wants me to hear. To react. I don't let him down.

I am dripping wet. I grab a towel, unlock the door and look out. He is just about to leave, suitcases packed. He gives me a dark look of injured victimhood mixed with triumph. Far too late I realise what has happened. How deeply I have been manipulated.

He wanted this. Stupid, stupid, stupid me. All this time he had been provoking me to get me to react. At last, he has gotten what he wanted. He can walk away, go to his other woman and say I said those things, tell her how horrible I am. Say that I ended it by twisting the meaning of my saying 'this ends now'.

He walks out. The victor.

The door slams shut. His footsteps retreat. The car starts and he drives away.

Water drips from my hair, slides down my skin, pools on the floor. The truth settles around me. A death shroud. It will only be a matter of time before I am utterly destroyed. He promised what would happen when he left me. He would take all. I would have nothing.

I call him, so great is my fear of the annihilation he promised that I cannot help but try to stop its unfolding, but the narrative has already shifted to another, more sinister one. He accuses *me* of the things he had done *to me*, my pain and suffering usurped by him. When I protest, I am told I am crazy, that all I ever did was deny his reality. The line goes dead.

Alone, I wander through a house imprinted with the stamp of his hate, his words slide from the walls, the floors, the ceilings and doorframes, they reach out to me, catch me in their grip. Possess me. Enemies. Friends.

Here, in front of the staircase, on my knees I am a worthless shit, and a stupid cunt. Here, in front of the chest of drawers I am jealous of the other woman. I say no I am afraid for her and her children. I am shoved against the drawers, bent over backward, his big, beautiful hands around my neck, choking me. It hurts. I can't breathe. I rasp. 'Do it. Let it end.' He tightens his hold a little longer then throws me aside, a doll.

You get up. You always do. What else is there to do?

I process through the house. There is no escape. Every centimetre of it drowns in words and acts designed to break another human being. And I am not strong. I am a mess. I am broken. I know he has won. He knows he has won.

I blame myself. Because I fought back, I now face the ultimate punishment. Banishment. Poverty. Homelessness. And so, on Midsommar Eve, as all of Sweden celebrates the longest day of the year—as I later learned he and his parents enjoyed a barbeque, ate strawberries, drank beer and whisky and planned my demise, I walk, lost, frightened, and utterly alone in the house that will be taken from me. I can't bear it. The horror of it all. The unreality. I have been discarded. I am garbage. Worthless. Everything he said about me is true. I could not fix it.

By ten pm the anguish is unbearable. The facts glare at me, cold and precise.

I haven't worked in a real job in years because that was his wish, to control all, to provide for me, to be the man, as if we lived in some perverse version of Gilead, where he was the Commander and I his powerless, imprisoned wife. I cannot understand Swedish enough to work, because I have lost my hearing. Even with hearing aids, I cannot hear what is gone. I will have to leave the country. I cannot cope. I don't know who I am—what I am without him—without his abuse. I am utterly lost. I have no power, no agency, no control over my fate. I am completely dependant on him. He has everything in his name, the utilities, my car, the house, even my phone number.

As the daylight drags on and night refuses to fall, I stand in the hall, unmoving, and stare at the door. Will him to return. To come back and make the nightmare stop.

But this was not like when he wanted to go to a party. This time he is gone and will not come back. His wealthy mother came in her designer golf clothes and told me so earlier that evening. Already they were preparing for the next Act. The one where I am disposed of as efficiently and cheaply as possible.

My thoughts become treacherous. They entice me to end it all, to escape, to deny him the pleasure of my suffering.

Do it. If you don't do it now, you will do it later. It won't be worth staying alive. It will only get worse from here on out. Save yourself the suffering.

For two hours I fight. Debate the truth of it. Dwell in despair. See my future with striking clarity. I know my husband too well. I know what he is capable of. He will not see me right, will not wish me to have a chance at a new life. A good life. To find love. To be loved. My ruin is all he wants, hungers for. He reminded me often enough: If you are not with me, you will have nothing.

And so it begins. The beginning of nothing.

PART II | THE HUNTER

THE INSATIABLE VOID

Were there signs? Of course there were. Subtle ones and others... not so subtle. But there was always the doubt. That comes right from the start, planted within you, a poisonous seed that flourishes in the fertile soil of your beautiful, empathetic heart. Nourished on your goodness, it suffocates the truth and chokes your heart with lies—lies you think are truths. *Their* truths. It's amazing how fast it happens. I sometimes wonder if Black Ops agencies who turn people into killers use the same strategies. It's effective. And fast. They could learn a lot from narcissists. Maybe they have.

And it is done so expertly, so naturally. That large measure of injury and guilt they ladle out for your having even considered such a thing of them when you ask for clarity. Because in the early days, before they have groomed you to think as they do, see as they do, you will ask questions because shit won't make sense. I promise. Pay attention to that. Or don't—and end up like me. Your choice, but it won't work out any better for you if allow yourself to fall into the iron-gloved clutch of a narcissist. You lose. Always.

Always.

Engrave that onto your heart. You will lose. Get out early and you will lose far less, but you will still be battle-scarred. You will need therapy and the intervention and support of friends and family. Your instincts will be fucked and trust will be in very short supply. That's the light version. Get out too late, and you can lose all. Everything. Perhaps even your future. Don't be that woman. Don't be me.

Early in the game they hand you the baton to do their dirty work for them, because it is a game. It is not love. Even if it looks like it, it's not. It's a lie. A mirage of love. A fantasy. You get close enough to it, and it vanishes. It's ephemeral.

And so, transfixed by their narrative, you carry on witnessing the signs as they become more obvious. As they yell at a waiter for bringing the dinner they ordered, blaming them for having heard them wrong, when you remember hearing them order that exact dish.

But then, perhaps you didn't hear it right after all. He is so convincing in his outrage. You see the waiter's uncertainty, their humiliation, their eagerness to escape. You want to pity them, but that would be a betrayal to the one who owns you so you look down at your food and resign yourself to eating a cold dinner because you must wait for your husband to get the dinner he wants to be brought to the table.

Later, you will wonder if it was all about control. That dinner was to celebrate your finishing a book. Maybe he wanted to see you eat your dinner cold, while he ate his hot. They offer to keep my food warm, but he answers for me, tells them no, it will be fine. They shoot a look at me, give me a chance to speak for myself, their look betraying how taken aback they are of my husband's control over me in an ultra liberal society. It is Sweden after all. Not Saudi Arabia. I agree, meek, grateful for once his anger is directed at someone other than me. I dare not oppose him. He is the king, the emperor, the ruler of my existence, the definer of my reality. It isn't beyond him to get up and leave me behind, abandon me in the restaurant without paying the bill. I don't dare tempt fate. I will eat my dinner cold and be glad of it. I will thank him after for treating me to dinner, because he expects it. I have learned that. Always express gratitude. Always. Even for the abuse.

You never know what a narcissist's motivations are. You can't know. Their minds are slippery, dark, evil, mercurial. Everything moves, shifts, morphs to their prevailing narrative where they are the victim in a world out to get them.

Their inner world is nothing like yours which thrives on trust, intimacy, constancy, communication, cooperation, nurturing others, and wanting what's best for your partner. No. I will tell you what to expect. It will be unpredictable. Because that is the root of power. And they like power. Absolute power. You can either give it to them willingly, or they will take it by force, through manipulation, gaslighting, blame, isolation, and eventually, deprivation.

Either way, you will lose. But if you fight them, you will lose much more. You will lose a part of yourself. Remember that.

But there is another way. You *can* see them for what they are. Although it is deeply unpleasant to force yourself to see what you do not want to see, if you want to protect yourself from these predators, you can develop and hone your instincts to sense when you are in range of a hunter intent on nothing less than taking your energy, your life, and soul for themselves, through manufactured drama, blame, victim-mentality, and lies.

They will go to Herculean levels to feed the insatiable void within them. You might think it is about *you*, that someone has seen what a beautiful person you are and wants to bring you into their life to love and cherish you and that is why they are chasing you, but no. It is never about you. It is about *them*.

You are nothing more than food to them. Supply. You are a thing, something to be used and disposed of when exhausted. At best you are a drug. At worst, fast food. They are incapable of love. But they are masters of faking what you need to believe looks like love to get what they crave.

So let's begin. Let us first look at the mask, and then piece by painful piece, let us unmask the monster hidden beneath, and see them as they really are, not as they wish you to believe.

This is going to hurt. Prepare for the ultimate betrayal of your senses, to enter a territory where everything you see, hear, and believe is a deception, a brilliant perversion of reality.

It begins before they even utter a word to you. It is that look. That laser look that pins your soul to their will. A form of hypnosis. It is the prelude. This is their siren song, and the beginning of your soul's fall.

That tentative trusting step you take towards their outstretched hand is when it begins. When they choose you as their next mark and offer you everything you have ever dreamed of.

Yes, this will hurt. Because this is where fairytales come to die, and hope ceases to exist. And we have only just begun.

First. The Mask. What they want you to see:

Charisma. Oh my god. They will have it in spades. So much of it. You will be addicted to it, bask in it. They will make you feel like the centre of the universe, *their* universe. And people will like them, no love them, admire them. Be eager to please them. There will be something alpha about them, even if they are not beautiful, or what people consider attractive. Their charisma trumps that. It's blinding.

When they focus their attention on you, there is no halfway about it. You *know* they will get what they want. They are arrogant like that, know you will fall, know you are already lost to their charms.

You will feel as if you have been chosen by a film star, or a rock star, or a tormented creative, or bad boy, or whatever it is that makes your heart go boom. If you have what they want, they will find you, and be that person you crave. I promise you. Like Liam Neeson in 'Taken': They will find you and they will kill you.

Whoever is your fantasy, that will be who finds you. When you possess the ultimate cocktail of bleeding empathy, loyalty, independence, honesty, friends, a social life, wit, intelligence, success . . . god help you if you are also what the world considers attractive. Oh my god, the more you have of these things, the more supply you can give, and the more desirable you are to them.

If you dream of CEO's, and you have what they want, there will be CEO's. Not because you are the ultimate CEO magnet, no, because they can smell your longing a mile away. Like vampires. They find you. You are food for them. And they are expert hunters. You mean nothing more to them than a Happy Meal means to you.

They will not take no for answer. Because they need you, like a heroin addict craves their next hit. They will stop at nothing to get what they want. What they need. And right now, they need *you*. Not you, but what makes you, you. They want to feed on that, only once they have you trapped and begin to feed, they don't return anything except doubt, sorrow, loss, grief, and the decimation of your Self.

And for those who walk in the world unaware of the hunters prowling among us—as we search, trusting others to be like us, kind, good, honest, looking for love, hoping for love, they sense what we long for. It's innate for them. And then they are there, as if by magic, or the Law of Attraction, or destiny, or whatever else you have been focusing your intentions on, offering you a drink. The rock star, biker bad boy, CEO, architect, doctor, scientist, artist, poet. Slaying you with their *look*.

It is a destiny of sorts, but there is no magic. It is calculated. The hunter always has the hunted in their sight long before the hunted is aware. That is how they succeed. How they feed. How you fall.

And now you're fucked, because it's too late. There is no warning. You are the deer falling to your knees with the arrow buried in your heart, and they, the hunter, who kneels to cradle your head, and gaze, worshipful, into your trusting eyes as your light dies.

You cling to them, your last connection to life, wait for them to ease the razor sharp lance from your heart, to save you. To heal you. Instead, your life bleeds out, stains your skin, soaks your hair, drips from your fingers. You wait. Hope. Right to the bitter, bitter end, you live in denial, until you reach your dying breath and realise the truth. They planned this all along. Your destruction. The arrow was driven there by their own hand. That is how powerful they are. They blind you to what they are, have the power to hijack your survival instinct. You have let them destroy you, because of a lie. Their lie. A beautiful, deadly lie.

They will make you think they love you, your whirlwind affair will drive you mad with passion, longing, and take your soul to places you never knew existed. You will fall asleep with your lips touching, and wake in the same position. The bond you will create with them will become the foundation for your future suffering, but this part, oh, this part is unforgettable. A dream, transcendent, glorious. The greatest love stories pale in comparison.

They will give you everything you need to fuel your fantasy as fast as you need it, a pusher, sending you deeper into your spiral of addiction. You will be caught in a fury of emotions more intense than the affairs of Anna Karenina and Count

Vronsky, Romeo and Juliet, Elizabeth Bennet and Mr Darcy, and Ralph de Bricassart's forbidden love for Meghann Cleary combined. You won't even be able to put words to it. You won't want to. It is too sacred. You are alight with life, with love, adoration. Hope. You believe all your dreams have come true. At last. You can't stop yourself, you fall deep and hard. None can resist such a seduction. None. So don't blame yourself if you now find yourself in a hell you can't even begin to understand or explain. You had as much power as that deer in the wood when you were targeted. The hunt is always in their favour. They make sure of it. They are calculated like that. It is their survival at stake, after all.

When they are in seduction mode, they give you an experience of passion and romance you will never forget—can never forget. You will never be able to erase it from your soul even after years of humiliation and abuse. It is that potent. It paralyses your senses and its imprint lasts forever. It is so powerful it will eclipse romantic encounters in your future. Why? Because what they gave you was a lie, a fantasy, a fabrication, and real love, real men, real relationships are flawed. That *je ne sais quoi* is not there, because it not poisonous. But once you partake of the narcissist's poisoned fruit, everything after tastes bland, dull, boring even. But we will come to that tragedy later.

For now, it is enough to understand real relationships are not staged, every detail controlled to ensure a long feeding and you always doubting, blaming yourself, never giving up, never seeing what they are, because how it begins is what you crave, long for, fight to get back again. What you believe is real.

Until it's too late.

To continue. The mask. What they want you to see.

In the beginning, they listen. They are the *best* listeners, and are even better at asking questions—the right questions, the ones you long to be asked. The ones capable of creating deep intimacy in a real relationship. The questions most men won't ask, because they simply don't think like that.

You will think you have hit the jackpot, found the rarest of all men. So eager are you to share with them, a starved creature longing for the ultimate bond and, already impaled by their arrow, you willingly divulge everything to them, let them dig deep—never once suspect treachery, betrayal, deceit. You trust them. You love them. You feel loved, cherished, adored, worshipped. Eager to please them, to bond with them, you tell them everything. More than you have ever told anyone. It feels right. You feel close to them. They support you, say all the right things, encourage you to tell more. To tell all.

And you do. Eventually.

And what do you learn about them in these epic sessions of vulnerability? Lies. False narratives. Rewritten histories. Of course you do not know this at the time, you take their word for it, and what they say is so solid, so cohesive, it *feels* real. It feels like the truth. They are utterly convincing. They may even shed tears and let you hold them as they weep. Your empathy levels explode. You want to help them, to make their life perfect, to undo all the wrongs that have been done to them, this perfect, good, caring person who suddenly fell into your life and loved you exactly how you wished to be loved.

You promise to never leave them, to support them, to care for them. To heal them. To be better than their ex who hurt them so much. Than their parents who only wish to control them.

It can take years before you learn the bitter truth, that in those halcyon days you were fed half-truths, misrepresentations, and outright lies. Massive omissions surface through random conversations that inevitably come to you as these things tend to do. The history you were given morphs into a jigsaw puzzle of mismatched pieces from different puzzles, and the more you try to piece the truth together, the deeper the deceptions and lies go, until you have no idea what the truth is and you are lost in a 3D version of a dozen different puzzles none of which have anything to do with the other. You back away from the dissonance. It is unbearable. Because to face it means you have no idea who the person truly is you are with—who you sleep beside every night. You realise you know nothing about them.

Except for one thing.

They are liars.

DANCE OF DESTRUCTION

Narcissists are natural born storytellers, and their stories are impeccable. I am a writer who creates entire worlds, and can spot the most subtle plot holes miles away. And I didn't see the lie. Because the narrative was brilliant. If you take anything from this chapter, this is all you need to know: Narcissists are going to tell you a story you cannot help believe, fall for, become invested in and care about. A narrative you are going to want to have a hand in changing the course of. You will be dragged into their story, their lie, and give them all your time, energy and love in trying to turn their poisoned past into a happy, healthy future. You will fail. The intention is for you to fail. You must fail.

Why? Because their internal narrative is critical to their existence. These carefully tended orchards of poisoned fruit are nurtured with fanatical devotion because the narcissist's identity is not who they are inside, (because there is nothing inside, and they cannot bear it, so they create their narrative to block that void). No, their identity is their *story*.

And on this flimsy, fragile foundation they initiate relationships, seduce their targets, and begin the long process of siphoning away the energy, empathy, and love, of those they impale with their arrow of destruction.

Eventually, the things you were told they needed, the things you have spent months giving to them: the attention they craved, the support they never had—the love they didn't get returned to them—changes into something else. Your gifts, given freely, and in a spirit of love become something nefarious in their minds. *You* become the problem. *Your* gifts become the cause of their unhappiness.

When you try to understand, to recall the things you discussed, what they said, the answer is always the same:

No. I didn't mean it like that. You weren't listening. You never listen. If only you would listen, you would understand what I want. You are just like all the others.

And yet, even as they say these things to you, in a way that makes you feel guilty, that troubles you deeply, you *know* they were very clear, they wanted *exactly* what you have given to them. And they did. But not anymore. Because you are now threatening to dismantle their narrative, which is a terrible crime. You are threatening their very existence. It has to stop. And it will stop, by them taking you apart piece by piece for having done precisely what they wanted you to do.

Doubt hits you at the speed of light. You scramble through your memories. No. You can clearly remember in the beginning as you lay in each other's arms, they confided to you if someone were only to do x then they would be able to heal, could at last be happy—they made it sound so simple you wondered why no one else could have done that for them.

Perhaps they picked terrible people. You know you are not terrible. You are good. Kind. Driven by love and loyalty. Then you recall how you explored what they had shared, to be sure you had it right and had not misunderstood a thing. You learned precisely what they needed so you wouldn't hurt them like all the others had.

And because you love them, and want them to be happy, and because you want to bring your relationship back to that place where things were amazing, you work hard to please them, endure their moods, their sudden, inexplicable rages, their criticisms, complaints, and negativity because they are wounded after all. They need extra love and attention. And you have that to give. You are wired to give it. And they know it. That is why they chose you.

Deep empaths are unique; they are the only ones who have the strength to continue to sacrifice far beyond what anyone else could give. We tell ourselves if we just do this one more thing, just stretch ourselves that little bit further they will be better. That our endurance run through their gauntlet will all be worth it. You remember how good it was before everything turned dark. You have the benchmark. You were there. It was real. It can come back—if only you get this part right.

But you can't. It's *not* what they want. It's what they want you to *believe* they want. It's an impossible goal they set for you to waste your energy trying to fulfill, while they watch you, satisfied, and feed on the power they have over you to do whatever they demand. You are blind to it, caught up in your so-called noble purpose, which cleverly keeps you occupied from seeing who they are, and what they are doing to you as they chip away at your confidence, your kindness, your care. Your love. As they question your motivations, and make oblique remarks that perhaps you are doing to them the very thing those who came before you did to them. They wonder if they misjudged you, or worse, maybe you deceived them like the others did, and they made a mistake with you.

To be on the receiving end of this is brutal. Crushing. And they are so adept at what they do, as they plant seeds of doubt with veiled accusations, implied blame, your 'crime' described in a light that is utterly skewed from reality, that makes you wonder if you are losing your mind because they are so convincing in their hurt. Sometimes they cry. You feel like absolute shit. They won't accept your consolation and turn away from you. Cut you off. After all, you are the enemy now. You have a lot of ground to make up to get back into their good books.

Somewhere in the midst of their mind games (because that is exactly what they are), your gut protests, says the version they are pouring into you is not how it happened, that it is riddled with inconsistencies, misrepresentations and full-blooded lies. Where they are always the victim, and you the monster. Nothing is ever that black and white. You notice they take zero responsibility. Everything is on you. Always.

At this point, when you don't understand their *modus operandi*, you don't realise you are effective. Too effective. Your incredible ability to 'heal' them is a threat to their identity—to their narrative—because you are getting dangerously close to dismantling the story of their victimhood and their purpose to exist. So, their narrative slides to the side a little, the details alter subtly, and it's your fault for not getting it right the first time. They begin to undermine your worth, mock the depth of your effort, perhaps even apply a little light punishment for good measure. An hour or two of silent treatment. It works. You get the message. You misunderstood what they wanted. They are hurt and it's your fault. You feel like total shit. A failure. Unloved. They are very good at making you feel like garbage, and teaching you they hold the power to reprieve you from that awful place.

You resolve to do everything you can to prove to them you are not like those others. To undo the harm you have clearly done in your overzealous attempt to make them feel loved and cherished. To make them feel like they matter and are important to you, unlike those others who only used them for their own selfish purposes.

You deepen your efforts. You cook their favourite foods, bake for them, go to the bakery on the weekend while they are still sleeping and buy fresh croissants, keep them warm them in the oven so when they wake up the house smells gorgeous. You ask what they want to do and do that, even if what they want to do doesn't include you, that's OK. You can do other things. You just want them to be happy. You stay behind and wish them a good time while they go out and do their own thing without you—and hope it proves how little you ask of them. How you want them to feel good and liberated with you, unlike their ex who demanded they spend all their time with them.

Of course, no matter what you do. You are still wrong. It gets worse. The recriminations. The narrative shifts again. You are now officially the problem, the cause of their unhappiness. You try another tack. You leave them alone, do the minimum, because they say you annoy them. And now you are wrong again. You neglect them. You cannot ever make it right. You can never make them happy. Because for them, the only pleasure they get is from dispensing psychological pain, watching you suffer, and nursing their narrative of victimhood. They change the rules, and suggest maybe you are crazy when you say that's not how you remember things. You believe them. You start to think maybe you are crazy, because the only thing that is consistent is the inconsistency, and they, the ones in full control of the narrative.

And you don't ever see the truth. Ever. You fall deeper into shame, into worthlessness, into despair. You want that life back you had at the beginning, but it's so hard, so elusive. Always on the horizon, a mirage that vanishes the moment you reach it.

And when you are in the midst of this unstable, ever-changing place, you internalise their blame, accept the 180 degree shifts in their narrative, because there is always a reason, and it always points straight back at you. It's a lot to bear. Especially when all you have done is what they asked. And now, you are wrong. Again. It makes no sense. Your thoughts cycle round and round seeking a safe haven, a single place of certainty in a place of constantly shifting sands.

You won't find it. The closest you will get to safety is through creating dissonance within your Self, through internalising their blame and taking total responsibility for the unhappiness in your home, for their mood, for their anger, for their punishments.

This betrayal is perhaps the single most destructive thing that happens to you in your soul's death spiral. It is the beginning of the fracture you create inside your Self to make all the broken pieces fit. It is where you lose yourself, and the hell begins.

To recap. The key components of a narcissist's mask: charisma, and a presence that blindsides your senses, even if they are not what the world considers attractive, they will be attractive, I promise. They will drive you to heights of passion, and be the best listener. They will want to know everything about you. No, not your favourite ice cream flavour—your vulnerabilities, your deepest hurts. Your traumas. Your weaknesses.

They are convincing storytellers of a past filled with injustice and hardship, of bad people doing bad things to them (these will be women, their mother, exes, and/or female bosses in a cleverly couched campaign of misogyny that will be so convincing you will start to wonder if feminism has gone too far if men must suffer so). But, they say with a reassuring smile, at last they have found you and you will make it all better. You are not like them. You are different. Special.

Your empathy levels will hit overdrive. This alone should warn you that you are in the presence of a predatory narcissist looking to secure their next supply. They are not a stray cat huddled outside your window, their eyes huge in their head, half-starved and begging to be let in from the cold. *That's* what those levels of empathy are for. For helpless creatures in dire need of survival. Not for grown men with jobs, and a functioning life who hit you with a laser look across a crowded room. No one in that situation deserves that amount of empathy. No one. And if they are triggering this reaction in you. You are being controlled. You are being baited, hooked, and reeled in. Your window to escape with your soul intact is rapidly closing.

There is one more component to their mask, which has been left to the last on purpose. It is the most important one of all because it can save your life if you are sharp and paying attention, it's the one component that overlaps the divide between the mask and the monster. You need to remember this one, brand it onto your heart and your mind and cling to it, because it is the most obvious one of all.

When it happens. Run. Get out. Fast. Excuse yourself, go to the washroom and never come back. If you are in another country on holiday with them (like I was) pack your bags and get the first flight out (I didn't). Because this single component is guaranteed to give away the truth of what they are if you are switched on enough to see it. It's glaring, and even when in seduction mode it will happen. Of course, there is the narrative soon after, the justifications, the indignance, the blame. If you let them pour their lies into you, their manipulations, it will be too late. Actions. Actions are what matters here. Not the words.

Especially not the words that come after.

Nuremberg, Germany. Summertime 2009. He drives his BMW rental around the city looking for a place to park. It's the seduction phase. I bask in how wonderful he tells me I am. How perfect. How I am everything all the others were not. He spoils me. Sends me to spas for massages and beauty treatments while he goes to meetings. Takes me out to dinner. We eat breakfast together holding hands. I exist in a haze of blissful happiness. Everything is perfect.

He still drives, searches for a place to park so we can go out for dinner. Everywhere is blocked by locked bollards, and places reserved for permit holders. We pass one historic building after another. It's an enchanting city. Cobblestones, medieval walls, cathedrals, plazas. I can't wait to explore it. With him, his hand in mine. His beautiful strong hand. I love him. So much. I look at him and tell him so with a smile.

He glances at me, but doesn't smile back. Tension radiates from him. His grip on the steering wheel is tight, even though we are not driving fast. Behind his Hugo Boss sunglasses, his eyes are narrowed, scanning the streets for a place to park. I sense he doesn't want me to speak. I take the hint, and reason he must concentrate. There are a lot of one-way streets after all. It's an old city. A maze. I turn my attention back to the window, spot a few places I hope we can see. One restaurant looks particularly nice, with a beautiful terrace, and white linen covered tables surrounded by perfectly clipped boxwoods in planters. Maybe we can eat there.

We turn another corner and ahead I see the entrance to a multi-story car park, the entrance barricaded by the standard striped panel and a machine to collect a ticket. I am secretly pleased. It is very close to the restaurant. It will be so romantic to dine there. A beautiful memory I will cherish. I can't wait. I drop the visor and check my make up in the mirror as he pulls up to the machine.

I could use more lip liner and lip gloss, I think. I want to look pretty for him. I dip into my cosmetic bag and take them out.

'Fuck!'

It startles me. This sudden, angry outburst. Fear touches me. He sounds scary. I stop what I am doing and cut a look at him. His breath is tight. His nostrils flare. He stares straight ahead, past the barrier into the enticing depths of a half-empty car park. He glares at it with pure hatred.

'It's for permit holders only,' he snaps, as if it's somehow my fault. I feel like it's my fault, the way he says it. 'This fucking place. Fucking Nuremburg. Fucking Germans.'

He rams the transmission into reverse and backs up, fast and hard. His anger hot in the roar of the engine.

I glance into the side mirror. There is a car right behind us, waiting to enter the car park. I open my mouth to warn him.

We slam into the car behind us. I surge forward. The seat belt catches me. It hurts. I blink back tears of shock. Glimpse my pale reflection in the mirror of the visor. The lip liner and lip gloss are gone, lost to the footwell. I wait for him to check on me. He doesn't.

'FUCK!' He pounds his palm against the steering wheel. 'Fucking asshole. Couldn't he see me there?'

My body reacts faster than my mind, which is slow, caught in the treacle of disbelief, of a dream turned into a nightmare in the space of a heartbeat.

Like a deer blinded by the headlights, I freeze. Fear pours through me. The man beside me is big, strong, and very, very angry. I hold my breath. Say nothing. Wait. Hope he doesn't turn on me.

He turns in his seat and gestures at the car behind him to back up, impatient and rude. Whoever they are, they do. They both pull to the side.

He shoves the car into park and leaves, taut with rage. The door slams so hard the car shakes. Never once has he asked if I am alright. It is if I no longer exist. In a way I am glad. I don't want his attention on me. I don't want him anywhere near me.

Even though he is outside, and I am in the car, I continue to hold still, afraid to move, paralysed by the suddenness, the insanity, the enormity of it all.

My thoughts tumble together, replay the event in all its impossible, incomprehensible ugliness. He didn't look into the mirror before he backed up. I saw it. He just stared into the car park and then hit reverse. He backed up into the car behind us and now he is mad at *them*. I wonder of they are hurt. I wonder if the police will come. I wonder about the damage.

I watch the altercation out the window, he is gesturing, furious, at a middle-aged blonde woman. He points at the entrance to the car park, at her, then at the rented BMW. He is yelling, it's easy to tell. His hands curl into fists. I am scared he might hit her. She cowers. He shakes his head, looks at her in disgust, strides back to the car, and yanks open my door and leans past me to open the glove box. He says nothing. Ignores me. I sit completely still. The glove box lid hits my knee, hard. I don't move. Don't make a sound. He grabs some papers from the folder inside and leaves, slamming the door behind him so hard my ears ring.

The lid to the glove box is still open. I consider closing it, then decide not to and rub my knee instead. Maybe he wants it left open for when he comes back. I unbuckle my seatbelt and ease forward to collect my lip liner and lip gloss from the foot well and place them back in my cosmetic bag. For some reason their presence embarrasses me, as though they mock me for what they represented. Everything feels far away. Distant. Unreal. Only minutes ago I was about to fix my lips to look pretty, thinking about a romantic dinner in Nuremberg with the man I adored, and now . . . this. Whatever this is.

He returns. Eventually. I tense. Prepare myself for whatever will come next, more yelling, more swearing, more hitting the car's steering wheel . . . I don't know. All I know is I am stuck in the middle of Germany with a man who has serious anger issues. I think about my exit strategy. I'll keep a low profile, not attract attention, not ask questions. When we get back to the hotel, I'll check my phone and pretend regret that urgent work has come in and I need to get back to Copenhagen sooner than expected. So sorry. And I was having such a good time. I'll say all the right things. Anything to get out. Platitudes I hope he'll believe. I'll pack, get a taxi to the airport, and take the first flight out. I will cut contact. Whatever we have had, it's been ruined by this. I am scared and I want out.

The other woman leaves, but doesn't go into the car park. As she drives past, she is crying, her makeup smeared under her eyes. He settles into his seat and pulls the door closed, doesn't slam it, just closes it like a normal person. Calm surrounds him. He reaches past me to collect the leather folder in the glove box and puts the papers back, neat and tidy. He sets it back inside, perfectly aligned, and shuts the compartment.

He looks at me. Concern creases his handsome features. He catches my hand. Strokes the back of my knuckles with a tenderness I know well.

'You ok?' he asks, as if the other person caused the collision and not he.

I know what he is asking. Was I hurt? No. Not really.

But I wasn't ok. Not at all. I was scared. Of him.

I nod. What else can I do? I wasn't about to start a conversation about *that*.

I look out the window, think of the crying German woman. She was innocent. Her evening—probably the next few days—has been ruined because of him, because he didn't look in the rear view mirror before he hit reverse. Maybe she had plans tonight, but now her car is badly damaged, and she will have to deal with that. Worse, whatever transpired between them during the long interval of dealing with the papers has left her visibly upset. He did that. He made her cry. Why? I can't make sense of it. He was at fault. Everything was his fault. He should have gotten out and tried to make everything right, instead he went on the attack, used his strength and size to intimidate a woman weaker and smaller than he.

He sighs. A resigned thing. He pulls off his sunglasses and sets them aside. I sense he wants my attention.

Of course, I give it to him.

He reaches out to catch my chin in his hand. His eyes move over me, missing nothing. He can smell my fear, I can tell.

'I scared you, didn't I?' Gentleness oozes from him.

I don't expect this. Am caught off guard. Know it's pointless to lie.

So I nod again. I don't trust myself to speak. I just want to get back to the hotel, get my things and leave.

'I am sorry you had to see that,' he says.

See what? I want to ask. See him lose his shit? See him totally fuck up and take no responsibility? See him ignore the harm he did to me, two cars, and intimidate the woman he had wronged?

Instead I wait, to see what he will say.

'You are going to leave, aren't you?' he asks, quiet. His hand is still holding my chin, forcing me to face him.

I have always been a terrible liar. I look away, but it's too late. He already knows the truth. He can see it all over my face. I'm out. So out.

'She took full responsibility,' he says. 'All this is her fault.'

I can't help it. The words fall out.

'You *reversed* into *her*.' I say.

He looks pained, as if my words physically hurt him.

'My car wouldn't have touched hers if she wasn't so far up my backside. I saw her and had time to brake. She admits she was too close. Technically, she rear-ended *me*.'

Technically. I blink. I literally don't know what to say to this. He was at fault. No one reverses without checking behind them first. He didn't check. End of story.

Who will pay for the damages, I ask. Her or him? He says his rental insurance will cover everything. Even though she admits she is at fault and agrees not to involve the police, he has offered to get his rental insurance pay for it, because people make mistakes sometimes. He makes it sound so magnanimous of him. I ask if he will be penalised by the rental company. He says no, that he is not worried, he has excellent coverage. He doesn't look worried. He looks calm. Content. I ask if there is damage to the rental. Nothing serious, he says. BMW's are strong. He smiles.

'Let's put this behind us,' he says. 'You must know it's not you I was angry with, but her.'

I can't keep up as he rewrites history faster than Stephen King writes bestsellers. I close my eyes and remember him being tense before she turned up. The rant about Nuremburg and Germans before he reversed the car in a fit of temper. Who was he mad at then? It felt like me—like it was my fault we were in Nuremburg and he couldn't find anywhere to park. It was his idea. He offered to bring us here. Said I would like it. And yet . . . I still felt to blame when things got weird. At least, until she showed up and he went full frontal on her.

'You aren't seriously going to make a big deal out of this, are you?'

There is ice in his question. I open my eyes and meet his. Catch the warning flickering in their depths.

'Are you really going to ruin our time together over a stupid woman?'

Stupid woman.

I can't answer. I have no answer. The atmosphere in the car thickens incrementally. He lets go of my chin and starts the car.

'Fine. Have it your way. I'll take you back to the hotel so you can pack, then drive you to the airport. A taxi would cost a fortune.'

He reverses the car. This time he checks the mirrors first, at least. He shoots me a tight look. 'Thanks for ruining Nuremburg,' he says. 'I was looking forward to showing you around.'

I can't keep up with how fast the narrative is changing. Now *I* am in the wrong. I am the problem, and he is hurt by *me*. My stomach clenches. Anxiety eats me. I can't think straight. He drives. Slow, purposeful. Past the restaurant I had hoped to dine at with him. He is calm as death. I say nothing as we leave the city and drive alongside the beautiful, red-tinted medieval walls shutting us out from where our afternoon started so differently—from where, in a parallel reality he found a parking spot and we are sitting down to a romantic dinner in that elegant restaurant and ordering wine, in a reality where none of this has happened.

I feel punished. I feel bad. I start to wonder if I saw it wrong, maybe he did see her and I missed it. Everything happened so fast. Uncertainty claws at me.

He drives in silence. He doesn't look at me. It's as if I am invisible. It's horrible. Only ten minutes have passed. He is not driving fast, even though we are on the Autobahn. It's going to take much longer to get back to the hotel at this speed. I wonder how I will bear it.

The pressure increases. A vice. The minutes crawl by, cars pass us, some blast their horns, angry with how slow we are going. Panic touches my spine. I can't breathe. I crack. Anything to make the siege end. To bring back peace. I must have seen it wrong. I ruined our day in Nuremburg. It was that woman's fault, of course, I didn't see it right. I understand why he was so upset. Anyone would be.

He smiles. The atmosphere dissipates. Relief floods me. Later, as we eat dinner, he pours my wine and acts as though nothing happened. The badness shrinks, becomes compressed, an offence, unable to co-exist in this place of intimate harmony. It fades to grey, a bad dream—one I long to forget. He puts his arm around me and feeds me morsels of beef from his plate. Adoration and tenderness surround him. I am beloved. Cherished. Forgiven.

He doesn't take me back to the hotel until it's very late. By then I am too tired to pack, to leave. I decide to think about it in the morning. It's so complicated. I don't know what to think anymore. So I don't think. I let him hold me and tell me he loves me more than life itself. As I slide into sleep, I realise he never admitted he was wrong about anything. Not even for hitting my knee with the glove box lid. He kisses my forehead, and tells me he couldn't live without me. I reason he didn't hurt my knee that bad, perhaps he didn't even notice. It's not worth it to bring it up when things are so peaceful.

I close my eyes, bloodied and blinded by my own hand, and the final red flag he brandished before me rots and turns to dust.

PART III | OVERCOMING THE DARKNESS

RISE FROM THE CARNAGE

I miss the birds. The beautiful, elegant murmuration of jackdaws sweeping across dusky Swedish skies. How they would move in synchronicity, tie those complex invisible knots and release them, only to slide into another, even more complicated loop. How did they know what to do? Hundreds of them seething as one entity, as if they possessed one mind. Who led? Who followed? Or were they all followers and leaders at once? Were they aware what they were doing was utterly magical to witness, an otherworldly, haunting emulation of a living fractal? Probably not. They just did it. It was a wonder.

Being in a relationship with a narcissist is similar, in a twisted, ugly-beautiful way. You become one in a complex, endless dance that morphs and changes, yet never completes a cycle. Are you leading? Are you following? You don't know. You become an extension of them. Of their reality. Of their needs, wants, unhappiness, of their rules of engagement that shift and slide. You tumble after them, as the skies spin and the ground turns sideways, and the world becomes a blur—your only constant, the one who lifted you up to the skies and pulled you after them, driven by your desire to make it to stop, for it to end, to at last come to rest—and the brutal belief in the lie you have to power to do so.

And then they discard you, vanish as abruptly as they came into your life, their toxic wing beat eclipsed by the glare of a sunbeam. Lost, disoriented, purposeless, you continue your erratic flight through the sky, waiting for them to return, enslaved to their control. Neither leader nor follower, you struggle to maintain continuity in your solitary dance, but there is none.

Alone, you push on, the pointless, lonely twists and turns of your flight embedded into your behaviour, a siren call for help none can hear or see. You cannot cease what you have been trained to do, and so, unwanted, unloved, you plummet, an exhausted shell, locked in the silence of your vanquished soul, of a heart broken beyond repair.

And this is how it ends. This is what happens to those who stay, who do not escape—who cannot escape.

It is day twenty-one of my solitary month-long stay in Poland. I lost some writing days traveling, dealing with the ongoing court case, and on one particularly terrifying night and day, in a battle facing the depth of the consequences of having spent a decade in a narcissist's reality, and accepting just how much damage had been done—of just how much of my future had been taken from me, and what it would take to change that.

It is perhaps similar to when you decide to improve something in your home. Paint a wall, or replace a bathroom suite, and you think: I will just fix that and everything will be wonderful. But as soon as you fix that one thing, suddenly in its changed appearance, all the other things that were also in need of attention you couldn't see before become visible. And you can't unsee them. They bother you. Prey on your mind.

As you continue, go deeper, you see more things to fix, to improve, or to throw away and replace. It's overwhelming. If you had just left that wall alone, or the bathroom suite, you would not have revealed to yourself all these other things, some of them much worse than the problem. When you replace the bathroom suite, you learn the floorboards are infested with woodworm. When you lift up the floor, you discover mice. You keep going until your house is nothing more than a skeleton, a frame, and still, there are things wrong. The ground your house is built on is subsiding.

That is what is to come. I want to warn you. Eventually you will muster the strength to fix that one thing inside of you to make your life better, to reclaim your power, to begin to live again—and just like that house renovation, you will open the door to a cascade of buried trauma that will stun you. Trauma you will have forgotten. Trauma you thought you were over, and absolutely are not. And perhaps the most painful of all: the awareness of the depth of your brokenness. Because now, alone, without them there to cause stress and drama 24/7, the adrenaline stops and the pieces tumble into place. The dust settles. You find yourself alone, and surrounded by utter carnage.

This is what is to come. And I want you to know this, because no one warned me. No one. I was left to fend for myself through this. I will not do the same to you.

I hoped—no expected—writing this book would not only help others avoid the predators who walk among us, but begin to heal the fracture deep within my soul, and provide the foundation to build the bridge back to the woman I once was. Instead, writing this has ripped open a thousand doors to a thousand worlds of suffering where I was traumatised every day, constantly, until trauma became 'normal' for me. People told me I was strong to have survived what I had survived. Strong?

No. There is strength. There is shock, and there is survival.

In this, there was no strength. There was survival. Years spent locked deep in shock, the psychological and emotional pain numbed to oblivion. But the body never forgets. For years, it can wait. Buried. Waiting. Silenced. For this. For when it is time to pull out the poisoned arrow. And then it comes. All of it. At once.

When you need to be strong isn't when you are under attack. It is after, when you rise to your feet in the wreckage of what is left of your life. *That* is when you need to be strong. When you discover exactly what you are made of and whether you can withstand the amount of loss you have sustained. When you take stock and see how much of your soul, of your self, has been ripped away. When you need to salvage the last scraps of your resources to fight, despite being certain you have none. For a time, you will simply exist as the shock dulls and reality takes you into its harsh grip. After all you have endured, existing is enough.

And now, the hardest thing you will face: You will miss your abuser, the one who destroyed you, sometimes for a long time afterwards. At times, it will be overwhelming. You will feel like you are dying without them. You will want to contact them—you probably will contact them, and things will only get worse. And yet, it will feel familiar, the pain, the sorrow, the anguish.

But this is your trauma bond that is dragging you back to them, not *you*. Not the you that you were before they ever hit you with their laser look and dragged you into their abyss. That you who had not been conditioned to their control would not have contacted them. Ever. We need to get her back. And we will. But many awful things must be faced first. But take heart. I am here with you, doing this with you, going through this with you. I am not just writing this to you, I am living this with you. And it hurts. Worse than anything. If tears were currency, we would be billionaires.

You will crave the cycle of abuse because it will be all you know, you will think the abuse is love. It will have become your purpose to suffer at their hands, and if the poison has gone deep enough, it will have become your identity. To be their thing they torment. To exist in a horrifying cycle of redemption, accusation, punishment, suffering and reward. That familiar rinse and repeat to which you learned to adapt, which became a part of you, which you honed to perfection, as vigilant as an elite soldier. You have to cut that away like a festering abscess, and it's going to hurt, more than you can imagine, because what's left afterwards for a time is . . . nothing.

To navigate the corridors of their vicious, toxic narrative based not on reality—not on all the things you are being told you are doing wrong but on their need to feed on the misery they cause—you have to permit their poisoned arrow to pierce the depths of your soul. This is how the process of annihilating your Self begins. Of day by day, under an exhausting siege of gaslighting, denial, and intimidation you eventually succumb to their narrative and betray the senses you trust. You allow the narcissist to define what you see, hear, and feel. You ignore reality, make excuses to yourself, give noble justifications to others, make yourself smaller, and carefully bury all of the parts of you they dislike.

You do this for the sake of peace, for the hope of the life you had with them at the beginning to return. So, at first, though you resist, you realise in time it is less painful to accept their lies, their words—their definition of you. And they are relentless, the more you give up of yourself, the more they take. It is the most heinous of crimes. To be erased and remade, an automaton, a thing. And then, once you have been emptied of all, they leave. And the process begins again. With another. And they don't care if you know—if you see them giving another everything you spent years fighting to get back. It is the ultimate betrayal. It can destroy you. It is meant to destroy you.

The anguish of your aftermath will be unprecedented. It is a level of suffering for which you cannot prepare; where you will need to find the power within yourself to face each day like a warrior. You are in a battle against yourself, your thoughts and feelings treacherous, dangerous things, because they are *their* thoughts, buried in you, internalised by you. Lies. All of them. Lies you believe. Ugly words that defined you. Sometimes for years. This is the part that is going to hurt. So much. This is when, even though you are on your knees, you are weak, lost, broken and bloodied, you must rise and face this last, final battle to reclaim of what's left of your Self. And this can only be done by one person. You.

Strength. Now is when you need strength. You are done surviving. You are done being in shock. Now you are going to fight for your life. And I am going to help you.

BREACH THE BARRIER TO TRUST

Don't attribute to malice that which can be adequately explained by anything else. - Hanlon's razor

Let's begin with trust. The one thing you lost and need to regain to heal. Without it, everything is going to be much harder. Perhaps too hard. But to generate trust, you must be able to give trust—to let go to another and believe you will not be violated for doing so. You must have faith in what you cannot control, must believe it won't bring you harm. Easier read than done.

When you have spent any length of time with (or are still with a narcissist), your trust has been epically fucked. You have been disciplined not to trust what you see, hear, or feel and have relinquished your right to these things to another who has had a free hand in defining your reality, which is a lie. Their lie.

You have been taught to trust lies, and the layers go deep. Trained to deny the reality your senses feed you, you have forced yourself to exist in the narcissist's reality, a flimsy, shifting world that has crippled you. You trusted what they said, because it was 'safer' to do so. And now, they are gone and your survival instinct is to trust nothing. You exist in a place of fear and avoidance. Your friends and family say things to you, things you cannot believe, because you think they are lying. Because you were lied to, all the time. The gaslighting, the denials, the outright reconstruction of a past you were a part of into something completely different. Nothing feels real, and nothing can be trusted. This is what you know, and what you cling to. What was taken from you—and how it was taken.

Trust no one. Trusting someone got you here, so the safest thing is to never trust anyone, or anything anyone says again. Assume the worst. Assume they lie. Assume they are deceiving you. Assume you will be hurt.

Good plan. Right?

For a time perhaps, when you are at your most vulnerable—when you are reeling in your discard and not thinking straight.

Then . . . not so much. Then you run into difficulties. You don't trust your doctor, your counsellor, your friends, your family, or the nice guy who comments on your Instagram posts. You wonder if the customer service representative at your bank is being honest with you, and begin to doubt your lawyer who is fighting hard to defend you. You pull back from everyone, convinced they are lying to you, misleading you, setting you up so they can hurt you and take away what little of yourself you have left.

It's lonely, frightening, and alienating. Paranoia stalks you. It keeps you awake at night. Sometimes it will even wake you up. Fully formed conspiracies which makes total sense at 3am that keep you tossing and turning for two hours in gut-wrenching torment. You are hunted by your fears, by all the variables that can lead to pain. You can't make it stop. It's a nightmare. But still, better this than the alternative. To not know what is real. To be shredded to within a breath of your existence by another. Better to be defensive.

And so you don't trust anyone, or, if you are backed into a corner, you pretend to, but beneath your waxen smile, you fear the worst, prepare for the worst, think of ways to put up barriers, to claw back your autonomy, to never let yourself end up in such a scenario again. You don't want favours. Kindnesses are greeted with suspicion, because wasn't it kindness that trapped you in the first place? Everything is dangerous. Particularly kindness, and especially anyone who wants you to talk to *them* about what has happened to you.

Talking to someone is what gave them the power to manipulate and control you. No. Talking is definitely off the menu.

So you don't trust. You don't talk. You don't let people in. You keep yourself isolated, locked in your solitary prison because to come out is too dangerous. How long does this last?

A long time. If you want it to.

And then, when at last you are ready to creep up to the bars of your prison, to dare to cast a look outside, to risk unlocking the door, and take a step toward your freedom, you realise you don't know how to begin again.

Mistakes are made. Ones you must not blame yourself for, because you are a raw, broken thing, lost and alone trying to heal without a clue how to do it. Maybe you meet someone new and you let them in a tiny bit, out of loneliness, or just to prove to yourself you are better and you can handle human interaction. You don't trust them, of course. How can you? And so, things perhaps progress but eventually your lack of trust rears its head again, provoked by something minor, triggered by past events that led to great pain. And you react. Fed on years of deception, and driven by defensiveness, you nose-dive straight into destruction. You throw down the gauntlet, accuse them of what your fears have convinced you will come next and push them away hard and fast, believing it is for the best. Then you congratulate yourself on making a lucky escape. For a time you feel proud of yourself. Look how strong you are. You didn't get caught this time. You believe you have overcome your demons. For a while, at least. Then the doubts come back, worse than ever.

They depart, bearing the wounds you have inflicted without ever understanding why you reacted the way you did, and you are unable to explain. You can't explain. It just is. Silence falls. Maybe you'll try again, with another.

Maybe you won't.

Either way, eventually the truth arrives in all its ugly glory: No one will ever help you gain your trust back simply by having a relationship with you, no matter how good they are. The damage you have sustained is so deep no one will ever be enough to prove themselves to you. You will always find something to suspect, your need to protect yourself from more harm far outstripping your desire to be with someone, to give them the benefit of the doubt.

So you end up alone, before a solid wall that stretches to the infinite distance in all directions. An impenetrable barrier. You resign yourself to it. You back up, try another path, but all paths lead back to this wall. You see others arrive, remain for a time and then vanish. How do they do it? How do they pass through the wall? You wonder what is on the other side. You persist. And then you discover there is a hidden door.

And that door, is *you*.

To pass through that wall, you must trust yourself. Once you begin to understand this, you will discover trusting yourself is the only way you can build a foundation for giving genuine, healthy trust to others.

It won't work the other way around. You can't build trust in others by playing Russian Roulette with your future, by testing others against your (endless) suspicions founded on broken trust. Tests are a guaranteed path to pain. Nothing good comes from testing others. It cannot, will not work. It will not heal you and will never give you back the trust that was stolen from you. It will only cause you great emotional distress and pain, and potentially cost you good friends and relationships. This is broken trust at its most toxic. When what has been done to you spills over and hurts others. That is not the way. Even if it is tempting, and your defenses are sky high. Don't test others. Just don't. You will only hurt yourself more in the long run.

At any rate, if one's approach is 'guilty until proven innocent', how can anything valuable and worthy come of such contact? It can't. There is too much risk, too many possibilities for things to go wrong, and for your wounded heart to see malice where there is none. It is only a small step after a 'failed' test to reinforce the mistaken belief you cannot trust anyone ever again. Testing others is a path that leads to a lonely, empty hell.

So, let's get this part straight. No tests. This one is on us. We have to build trust in ourselves. And to begin, we must start with the tiniest of baby steps. Steps others might think are basic, but when you are deeply broken, basic is best.

Start with the GPS in your car or phone. If you are thoroughly traumatised you won't even trust your GPS. You will think it is lying to you, or not giving you the best route, or you will feel uneasy having a faceless entity know your plans and movements. Better to be invisible. Instead, when you must travel someplace new, you will double check maps online and memorise the journey in your head, or write it down on a Post-It perhaps days in advance. Anxiety is insatiable like that.

But, in reality, refusing to trust one of the most reliable tools in the world makes your life harder. Perhaps you weren't aware of construction along the way, or maybe you forgot a turn and now you are lost and have to pull over to consult your notes. Either way, not trusting your GPS is the hardest way to get from A to B.

So, start easy. Make a plan to go somewhere not too far, but also where you have never been before (this is important and will be explained why a little later on), perhaps a park, coffee shop, or bakery—just make sure to pick a destination you will enjoy. Plug it into your GPS. Follow the directions, even if your heart is thudding with anxiety and you are sure you are getting lost, stick it out. If you start to panic, tell yourself you can always backtrack. And if you do backtrack, it's ok. Try again the next day. Baby steps. It doesn't matter if it takes you a week to go four blocks, don't give up. You can do it. You will do it.

When you reach your destination, through trusting technology, you will cross a critical threshold in your recovery. The walls, floor and ceiling of your glass prison will waver under the force of your blow, cracks will splinter away, and spiderweb in every direction. This is how it begins, how you break the cycle of fear and distrust and give yourself the chance to foster the hope that perhaps not everything outside of you is going to hurt you. This simple, effective step is how you begin to break free of your long, lonely silence—how you start to find yourself again.

The next day, do it again. Go to the same place, still using your GPS but notice the journey a little more this time. Look at the nice buildings along the way, note the gardens, signs, shops, whatever takes your fancy. Consult your GPS but don't keep your attention glued to it this time. Let go, just a tiny bit. Breathe. Trust yourself. You will arrive, just like you did yesterday. Trust the GPS. Trust yourself. You got this.

When you get to your destination, reward yourself. Buy yourself a nice cup of tea or coffee, perhaps a pastry, or ice cream and stay awhile. Sit on a park bench or at a cafe, and just absorb the enormity of what has happened. Of what you have done. You gave your power up to something else and it didn't betray you. Instead, it helped you. It took you someplace nice. You discovered something new, had an adventure. A nice one. And now, you have a new place to go that is all yours, where no memories from the past can taint your experience. This moment is yours. All yours. Savour it. You have earned it.

Earlier, mention was made of taking yourself to places you have never been before. Going to new places has a doubly positive effect as you work to rebuild trust in yourself. First of all, going somewhere new means you are making new memories just for you. Second, you don't know the way, or exactly where to park, so you will stretch yourself by placing your trust in the GPS, and being rewarded with the reinforcement of continuous success. In addition, you open yourself up to experiencing little things you can't plan for, like perhaps the coffee shop only takes cash and you need to locate an ATM. Each of these small details offer you the chance to rediscover the resources you possess to resolve these minor obstacles.

Have you found a parking spot in a part of town you have never been? Take a moment to congratulate yourself. You need to get cash? No problem, you can handle this. You check your map, find the ATM and get the cash. You did this. You solved this. You trusted in yourself to overcome these small obstacles. Minor things to many, but enormous to those who have lived in fear and anxiety for far too long.

And it is a big deal. You are building a solid foundation of trust in yourself. No longer will you wonder if you can trust others, all you need to do, for now, is focus on trusting yourself, and know you have the skills to take care of you. Celebrate this shift. Mark it in your calendar. Because from this point forward you will gain strength in your self-trust as you increase the boundaries of what you are willing to relinquish, in what you will trust in, and in the chances you will take.

Each day, as you feel a little stronger, as the glass walls of your prison fragment and the fresh air of a new life beckons, give yourself more power to trust. Go for a walk in a forest and follow a marked trail. Trust the marks. Complete the trail. Celebrate. Do it again with a different trail on another day, but this time enjoy the scenery. Take photos. Mark your progress with selfies. Notice the change in your eyes, in their brightness, and in your posture as you immerse yourself into a different rhythm, one where you are in charge, and are giving yourself the tools to build trust in yourself.

In the beginning, trust in street and park signs, GPS, trail markers, and so on. Things such as these are guaranteed not to harm you. Go to a museum and lose yourself in its depths, then find your way back without checking a map, or asking for directions. You will do it. You will find your way out again, because you will have noticed things along the way: that statue of Ramesses, that painting by Picasso, the medieval knight on an armoured horse, whatever, you will remember and you will celebrate with a gift to yourself from the gift shop to mark the day.

Doing these kinds of exercises teaches you that you can trust your senses; that what your eyes have seen is true, real, can be depended on. You are re-discovering the world, in all its true constancy, its firmness. Your trust in your place in the world grows. You belong. You matter. What you see, hear, and feel is real. You experience greater freedom as you realise your senses don't lie, and the barriers that surrounded you collapse in the face of a world of solidity. Of facts. Of reality. One by one, the lies die.

It is a miracle, this part of your recovery. To learn to trust yourself again. It's extremely cathartic to keep a diary or document your journey in a private social media account where you can easily upload photos and write your experiences in real time.

Pay attention to how you change. It is so important to document this. You need to see your transformation, because there will be a transformation. And it's a beautiful thing. Perhaps the most beautiful thing you will ever witness. This is your re-awakening. Your healing journey into a new you. Another you. And it will be another you. The woman you were before you were targeted is gone. But the woman you are becoming is so much more. You will never be targeted again. Not if you give yourself time to heal, if you give yourself the chance to open the door in the wall that has been holding you back and you can move past it into a world where you can begin to trust others, slowly and surely, because you can trust what you see and hear as the truth.

When you are ready, if you can, take yourself on your ultimate journey. Travel to another country. Somewhere you have never been before. Spend time with yourself. Make new memories. Do things you love. Immerse yourself in what it feels like to be alive, free, and able to trust your senses. And as you walk in a new place, and drink in the details of another society, remember who you were when you began this journey, and feel who you are now. You did it. It's time to walk through the door.

And don't forget to celebrate.

FIND LOVE. REAL LOVE.

If you are a survivor of narcissistic abuse, you will have likely chosen a long, voluntary period of physical solitude. Of trusting no one. Of at most, engaging in superficial connections, online flirtations you can end with the push of a button. But one day, it will come—you can count it—the longing to love and be loved again. Of being with a real, live human being, of feeling their warmth, their touch, their skin against yours. Of being held, kissed. Loved. Of kissing them back, holding them against your chest, your heart beating in time with theirs.

At times your longing will be overwhelming. It is human nature after all. We are not solitary creatures. We are social animals, as the multiple lockdowns and enforced restrictions of the COVID pandemic has tragically proven. Being alone for any length of time is unbearable for most. A handful will not mind it so much. But even the toughest will need to connect with another person at some point. We all need to experience love and connection eventually. No one is exempt. And when that need comes, it blindsides you.

It becomes all you see. Couples holding hands, young and old. Your friends suddenly finding love and flourishing. Your neighbours inviting you to their wedding. Films and shows, books and articles featuring love will pop up on your feed as if your online tech can hear your thoughts (or at least your conversations).

But for you . . . No one. You wonder if this is going to be it for you. No one to lay down beside ever again. Just you on your own for the rest of your life surrounded by a growing collection of cats.

Encouraged by friends, at last you give in and post a dating profile online only to learn the horror stories are in fact, true. It's a cesspool of married men looking to cheat, players who want to play, boys young enough to be your son looking for a sugar mommy, and all out perverts who write disgusting things they want to do to you that makes your flesh crawl. You retreat. The longing persists. Well, you reason, it's just a biological imperative. It will pass. These things often do. You feed yourself the usual platitudes as you prepare your morning tea: If I am meant to meet someone, I will. It will just happen.

Then, as you pour the milk you recall how you met your narcissist. That 'just happened'.

Hm.

For those of us recovering from the trauma of a narcissistic relationship we need to be extremely careful when it comes time to seek love again. Although, take heart, there are things you can do to prepare yourself, a checklist of sorts.

First, if you have not yet begun to fully trust yourself, your senses, and especially your instincts, ask yourself if you are truly ready to judge the potential of a future partner with a clear heart and mind. If you are not, get your trust in yourself right. This part is critical. You will need it for what comes next. Go back to the previous chapter and practice the strategies in there until you feel your trust in yourself strengthen. Until then, you are at risk of re-traumatising yourself. Please don't. You have come too far to lose everything now. In Part IV, there are more strategies to help you gain trust and strength in yourself. They are there to help you, to arm you and protect you against those who seek to destroy you.

It turns out narcissists leave a mark on their targets, which is a beacon to other narcissists. It says: 'This one is food.' Long after they are gone you will become aware of this phenomenon when other narcissists enter your life and circle you—hyenas scavenging for the scraps left from the alpha's feeding.

Of course, while you are still healing, it won't be the overt ones like your ex who come for you. Those will pass you over for other more bountiful, untouched supplies. But the others, the 'weaker' narcissists, oh, they will come in droves. These insidious so-called 'covert' narcissists possess enormous amounts of charisma, and can weave charming tales of woe, injustice, and suffering, sometimes with self-deprecating humour that totally blinds you to what they are. You begin to build a perverse bond with them. After all, you are wounded too. You have a lot in common. It feels familiar. You could fight to get better together. You like this idea. Nurture it. One point for them.

Except... it's only you who wants to get better. *They* don't.

As you embed your time into them, you become caught in their complex web of problems, and are told how nothing gets better no matter what they try (and they make a great deal of noise about the trying part).

If you are unfortunate enough to have an expert covert coming for you, they will almost always have mysterious health issues no doctor can diagnose or cure, health issues they can talk about *ad nauseam*, and will use to excuse themselves from commitments at the last minute. And you can say nothing, of course, because if you do, you are an insensitive asshole. They are smart, these coverts. Like hyenas. Crafty. Yet despite all their manipulative skills, strangely these poor souls just can't get a break. Sigh.

They love it when you listen to them and offer helpful advice (which they will ignore as they continue to carry on doing the exact thing that got them in their mess in the first place). They *especially* like it if you make a big deal of their endless problems, and become outraged and offended at injustices done to them. There will always be some low-key drama going on in their life they will want to burden you with, and will need support to get through (though there will always be an excuse why they couldn't).

To make sure you don't run screaming for the hills, they will make sure to make you feel like you are helping them, making such a difference—how special you are. But no matter how much they convince you of this lie, do not be deceived. You are not making a difference, you are being used for the attention you are giving them on the one-way street that is their existence, and to vindicate their twisted, entitled narrative of specialness and exemption from responsibility (including giving an actual damn about you).

Over time, these subtler, less obvious narcissists are just as eroding and wearing as overt narcissists. Because they are difficult to pin down, you are again riddled with doubt. Are they using you? Are they really *that* helpless or just taking advantage? Do they have health issues or is it all an act? Are you being horrible for questioning their narrative? More circles. More wasted time. More lost energy. Another point for them.

These are the ones who are going to come for you in the wake of your narcissist's departure. Prepare yourself. Arm yourself with this knowledge so you can skip this part and see what they are right away. If you get hit within a week with the 1-2-3 of charm, charisma, and crap backstory, run. Hit delete. Block them. Whatever it takes. Cut them off. They will move on faster than you think. As soon as they know you won't play they will already be contacting the other irons they have warming in the fire. Save your heart for someone worth your time and energy.

So, who are the right people?

The ones who take it slow. The ones who want to get to know you in a paced and non-invasive way, starting things out as friends, nice and casual. They don't go straight for the pain and sorrow of your past by rummaging around in your closets trying to pull out the dirtiest laundry and wanting to go into every sordid detail. They want to talk about neutral things, test the waters, see if there are similar values and interests, if it's worth it to keep going.

They don't bring up their ex, past relationships or anything like that in the early days, or if they do, it will be just to say the facts. They tell the basics, and move on. They don't want to dwell on it, because it's in the past where it belongs. They will have been single for a while and not fresh out of something, or even worse, still living with their ex but 'broken up'.

Perhaps they have dated others since their last serious relationship. What matters is they are happy in their own company and in their own life and are not on the rebound. They are not looking for someone to rescue them (or re-home them). They are not someone who is looking to be with you for selfish reasons, because they are lonely, or just want a guaranteed lay. They are looking to meet a person they can share good times and weather the bad times. Equals.

And most importantly, whenever you have contact with them you will not be plagued by doubts afterwards. You won't be raking over everything they have said until you sicken yourself because it isn't aligned with what they said the last time you spoke. Narratives won't shift. They are constant. Stable. Sane.

There won't be any blame, or accusations of injury you have caused you don't agree with (or remember). You won't hear yourself apologising for things you didn't do just to keep the peace. Your instincts won't be firing in all directions warning you there is something dishonest about them, something you can't put your finger on, or just a general sense of wrongness about them that leaves you in a constant state of unease.

No. You will sleep well at night. No more tossing and turning. No more churning thoughts. When they talk to you, it's easy, uncomplicated, drama-free, and makes you feel better after, gives you energy instead of depleting it. That's what you want the next time around. That's the goal. Don't stop until you get it. You are worth it.

Go slow. Be patient. Be wary. Trust your instincts. Love will come. And this time around it won't be a lie because you will know the difference between what is love . . . and what is a lie.

Part IV | FOR THOSE STILL TRAPPED

IN HELL

You are there. Right now. In a place no one else understands. You are lonely, alienated, and hanging on to the thinnest of hopes: That if you just do what they want, everything will be better again. They will love you again. They will look at you with tenderness and adoration. God, you long for that. It's all you want. Just their love. Like before.

So you go on, nursing this fragile hope, even as they glare at you in uncontrolled rage and ravage your character, your body, your mind, your self with brutal slurs, words meant to hurt, with words meant to kill, barbed spikes of a whip; as they corner you when you try to escape, as they hurt you, leave bruises on your flesh, and fracture your fingers and bones when they throw you against the floor or into doors and walls—into anything that will hurt you, that will break you. Because they want to break you. All of you.

You beg them to stop. They laugh and call you worthless shit.

On your knees before them, you weep, and even as they raise their hand to hurt you again you tell them you love them. You. Love. Them.

They sneer at you and say: Too bad. And the hurt goes on. And on. Until you want to die.

For years I lived like this. Years. And for years I hid it. Denied it and took full responsibility for all that was wrong. I channelled my anguish into the love stories of my books and penned beautiful words of gratitude to my husband in the acknowledgements. Because without him, how could I afford to write full time? It was a double-edged sword. No abuse. No books. I romanticised it. What else could I do?

Oh how I loved him. Or, at least who I imagined he was. Because who he was in my mind was not who he was in reality. In reality he was a monster who hungered for nothing less than my annihilation. I still dream of him sometimes. Not nightmares, those I have in spades. No. Dreams where he is nice to me, like at the very beginning. I hate them. When I wake I face a fresh hell, all the feelings I longed for during those long, lost years return, pour through me, visceral, unlocked from the vault of the past in all their sensate beauty and I must overcome all the pain again. The loss. The longing. The unwarranted guilt. It hurts. All of it. It goes on and on.

It's a trauma bond of epic proportions. And you are still in it. Right now. For whatever reason, you are not ready or able to leave. You know best. More than any other, you know what your options are, what the consequences will be if you leave. You know because it's all you think about, day in and out.

Perhaps you are resigned to wait for the discard, because it will bring the least harm to you. Maybe you are waiting for him to replace to you, as he often tells you he will do, counting down the days to your liberation when another woman will take on the mantle of your suffering. A sister. A friend. You pity her, fear for her. You want to warn her, but you want to survive more. It's war after all. During the years you have suffered under his regime of hate, you have protected other women from him. You have done enough. It can be someone else's turn now. And so, you walk the darkest corridors of your soul and grieve, process past your carefully tended gardens of dead flowers. Of a life you never got to live.

Of a love that was a lie.

Below is a list of things I wrote to myself when I was deep in the trenches with my narcissist. I wrote these things to help myself survive what was happening. To give myself a guide I could refer to in times of chaos and crisis when my world was spinning. It helped. A little.

If you can, try to make a list like this for yourself that works best for your circumstances, to give yourself something to cling to when you are lost at sea. If it does anything at all, at the very least it gives a voice to what is happening. Be a friend to yourself. Be kind. Be supportive. For a long time, you may be the only friend you will have, so be the best friend you can be. Your life may well depend on it.

1. Don't engage. Don't try to establish any form of intimacy. Don't share your thoughts and feelings. He doesn't give a damn. If it's not what he is interested in, or doesn't give him supply, he will get angry, start a fight and make sure you know he is the victim. You

will end up having to apologize after a prolonged period of hostile silence. Be bland. Be neutral. Don't feed the monster. Stay out of his way.

2. Ignore the projection. Everything he is accusing you of is what he is doing to you. It's a lie.
3. Don't be baited into believing you are the aggressor. He's the aggressor. He is incapable of anything else. He will tell you he was never like this before you. He will tell you that you made him like this. He will blame you for his temper tantrums, destruction, and abusive behaviour. His will often remind you: 'If I wasn't with you, I would be fine'. But he won't be. He will never be fine. He will always be unhappy. He told you the same things he is saying about you, about his ex. It's a repeating narrative. He will treat the next person *exactly* the same.
4. Expect to be spoken to as though you are inferior, and in a bossy, demeaning manner. You don't deserve this. He will tell you how he expects you to react to what he says, and what he expects you to say to him (like you are a robot and not an actual person with their own feelings and views).

Expect those expectations to be wildly divergent with reality ie. you need to agree with 'his experience' of whatever he has built in his mind against you that day (he's the victim and you are the awful aggressor, so you get attacked), then you need to grovel and apologize, but in a way that pleases him, then you need to placate him until he feels better. Rinse and repeat.

5. Don't flatter him. It's what he lives for, if he is going to make you suffer day in and out, at least don't reward him for it.
6. Don't praise him either for the same reason. Just be quiet. Be silent. Don't attract his attention.
7. Don't disagree with anything he says no matter how disconnected it is from reality. You will never be heard or understood. He doesn't care. He will literally make things up to shut you down. See him for what he is: a man who wants to torture you for his own sick reasons. Don't be fooled by the skin he's in. He's a monster and wants to destroy you.
8. He will never be interested in your experience, your feelings, or anything he has done to harm you, and will NEVER be open to working through things with open communication. YOU ARE WRONG and HE IS RIGHT. This is fixed in stone, no matter what you do or say, he will never treat you respectfully, or as an equal. Ever.
9. Expect him to lie to you. A lot. Expect him to lie straight to your face denying what he is doing even as he is doing it.
10. He WILL be unreliable. He will not keep his promises. There is no point in mentioning it, because he is never wrong, and it is never his fault if he breaks his promises or lets you down. It's YOUR fault for 'nagging' him, and now it's punishment time, so now he won't do whatever he promised to do at all. In his mind, you deserve it.

11. He has no empathy. He is utterly incapable of it. At times he might act like he has empathy, but it is just because he is getting something out of it that benefits him. Give it enough time and you will learn it's temporal. It's all fake. He is a hollow person. A void. There is nothing inside him, no character, no honour, no experiences. NOTHING except a vampiric need to destroy the inner life and worth of anyone who ends up in a closed situation with him.
12. He will isolate you. He will never want to do anything fun or social. He will never suggest anything outside the narrow scope of his selfish interests (which are usually solo activities). Birthdays, seasonal holidays, etc will be just like any other day. Nothing special happens. Ever.
13. He expects full access to your phone, computer, paper files, everything. However, his will be locked and he will be devious with you. Expect him to cheat on you. If he can find a willing target he will take it. If his moods start to vacillate even more wildly than 'normal', it's not unlikely his current affair has turned sour, and he's mad, so he takes it out on you. Expect extremely abusive, irrational behaviour as he rages against the other woman for 'not doing what she is supposed to do'.
14. He lacks object constancy. If you are pleasing him, then he's all charm and kindness, tells you he loves you, wants to hug you, etc. If, two minutes later you somehow cross one of his invisible lines, then he switches instantly. He looks at you with pure hatred (even in public places)

similar to how a five-year-old glares at their mother when they can't have their way. He shouts at you, tells you he hates you, hates everything about you, can't stand you, and so on. Ten minutes later, once you have said whatever it is he needs to hear to undo the awful unwitting wrong you have committed, he loves you again. You are a thing to him, which either has a purpose or does not. He decides which you are, and there is no constancy. It's all about him, all the time.

15. He really, really believes his warped version of reality. It's scary. It never gets better, it only gets worse, and you pay the price with your soul.

16. Remind yourself he is an unreliable narrator therefore you cannot take at face value you are any of the things he is accusing you of, rather you are surviving a horrifying situation, and your goal is to get out and have a better life.

17. Do not keep silent. Don't hide what is happening to you out of shame or embarrassment. Do whatever it takes to connect with others. If you have isolated yourself from all your family and friends because of him, then join a Facebook Group. Start to tell people what is happening to you so you can hear their reaction and get another narrative to the one you are being fed 24/7. You need this balance and support to push back against the lies you are internalising.

18. Don't give up. Don't let him win. Fight with all your heart. You will survive this.

THE MOST DIFFICULT CHOICE OF YOUR LIFE

If you have not yet been discarded by your narcissist, you are in the unenviable position to make the choice to take control of your future and liberate yourself—to take away the pleasure they will get from throwing you away when you are no longer of any use to them.

But, this is not an easy decision, because it also comes with huge ramifications to your Self. It is not as simple as packing up your bags and leaving to stay with a friend or family.

They will come after you. They will not let you go because in their story only *they* can end things. *They* must discard *you*, and if you deny them this you will be in for a rough ride. You know this instinctively. You know if you leave, you will have to disappear and keep your head down until they seek out new supply and forget about you. Depending on your circumstances (and the depth of their desire to exact revenge) this could take time.

It's a logistical, emotional, and psychological nightmare, and that's if you are childless. Add in the complexity and legalities of child custody (and they will fight you hard for your children in most cases, not because they want them, but because they know you do and it's a way to hurt you and make you suffer plus burden you with expensive court costs).

So, it's not surprising so many of us simply shore up our dwindling reserves and batten down for another day of hell. It's simply the lesser of two evils. If you are in it right now, you get this. And it's heartbreaking that you do.

Planning to leave creates a deep sense of panic, of how you don't know who you are without their abuse and control, and in the realisation you have lost many of the basic skills to live like a normal person since they control every aspect of your life. You are terrified. And you are right to be, because they have taken almost everything from you. Leaving is just the first step in a long and painful recovery. And you know this. You are not wrong to hesitate. It's a huge choice.

You may have invested half your life into this person, have children with them, grandchildren even. You have been converted to their narrative cult, and to leave means not only will you lose a massive chunk of your past, but also a huge part of yourself. You don't know who you will be without them. It's the ultimate psychological injury, comparable to the Pit of Despair.

In the 1970s, a terrible experiment was done to baby rhesus monkeys. They were placed in total isolation in a V-shaped cage with only a narrow base at the bottom that slanted to collect their waste, and a mesh wire lid at the top. The cage was small. At first the babies would struggle to climb to the top for the chance to see outside their pit but would lack the strength to remain and would slide back down into the pit. After several days of attempting contact they would remain huddled in the corner utterly unresponsive. Some starved themselves to death. For those who survived this horrific ordeal—which, for some, lasted up to one year—it was discovered when the cage was at last opened and they were allowed out, they did not react at all to their liberation. They simply remained where they were, huddled, locked in misery and unable to accept anything would be better once they left.

And this is why so many of us *don't* leave. Because we don't believe it will be better if we go. Because they have told us if we do, they will destroy us for telling everyone 'our lies'. And we believe them, because we know what they are capable of.

Anyone who has not gone through the calculated, long-term trauma narcissists dish out behind closed doors will ever understand this. You can try to explain, even show them this book, but without having their worth, value, purpose, and identity eroded in a systemic campaign of psychological destruction they can *never* understand what it is to exist in this kind of sustained misery and devaluation. They just won't, so don't waste your energy trying to get them to.

When you do finally break the silence and let people know the truth of what you are living with, these same well-meaning (yet blissfully ignorant) people will ask how you could have remained so long with such a person—they say if it was so bad surely you would have already left by now.

This is what you will face when at last you reach out to others for support. First there will be disbelief, because of course you have been pretending for years everything is fine to avoid worse punishment, and your narcissist will also have convinced anyone you both know they are the greatest husband on earth —and you the luckiest woman alive. Every step is a nightmare of check-mates.

Opening up grants you the double condemnation of both being caught in a narcissist's narrative, and having to explain why you had to go along with it to survive. You try to describe your trauma bond, something you barely understand yourself. It's not easy because nothing you say is remotely relatable to your listener. They might even look at you like you are a little crazy. After all, your husband is awesome. They wish they had a husband like that. No. They don't. But that is what you will face. Disbelief. Minimising. Perhaps they might even distance themselves from you, subtly suggesting you are the problem. Prepare yourself. It can get ugly.

Even if you do get a sympathetic listener, they still won't be able to ever appreciate the depth of your pain, or the gravity of your experience, or how it's been enforced little by little with punishments and deprivations until it has become your reality. They can't understand how much it is costing you just to open up and share what is happening, because you are finally taking that critical step in distancing yourself from the lie of the narcissist's narrative to speak your truth, and to validate your reality which is wobbly enough as it is. The *last* thing you need is for people to question you. To side with him.

Which means when you decide to reach out please be *very* careful in whom you choose to confide. Do not speak to anyone who also knows your partner through work, friendships, or even from neutral places like the gym. Don't talk to people you are certain don't like him. They are not safe either. There is always a chance what you have said will get back to him.

If you use social media be extra careful about what you share, and with whom you share it with, because anything can be screenshotted and shared. You need to confide in people you can trust, who won't betray you when you least need it.

It's not very appealing, but at the beginning, your best and safest options are doctors, counsellors, social workers, experts in trauma, psychologists, and professionals like this. You can also call Women's Hotlines and women's shelters to get free confidential support. Use them as much as you need. You are fighting for your life. You are allowed. Tell them what is happening to you in as much detail as it takes to get things straight in your head. You need this to process what has been done to you, to make sense of it. They won't ask you stupid questions or make awful assumptions to undermine your tiny steps to escape your Pit of Despair. They will listen to you and help you. And if you are planning to leave first: I salute you. It's a powerful choice.

Below is a list of things to plan and prepare for as you get ready to go. You need to be smart, because they are going to be smarter. The more you have organised and ready, the more knowledge you have, the more essentials you have prepared, the more powerful you are. And there is nothing like having the secret knowledge that you are preparing to leave when they are screaming at you, and telling you that you are a worthless piece of shit, and you know you are getting ready to leave. That's power. Many of these things I did even though I was discarded, so these tips come from personal experience. Sometimes just the thought and the act of preparing is enough to keep you going for another day, to keep you on your feet—even when they ram you into a wall and tell you they wish you were dead.

Your exit strategy preparation checklist:

1. Make sure all your paperwork is up to date and in order. Ie. Passport, driving licence, car ownership, pet registration and insurance is in your name, etc.
2. If you can, get a post nup if you haven't made a pre nup. Fence off what is yours, and make sure if you are a creative to protect your rights to your art so they can't come after you at a later date and demand compensation for what you created while living under their regime. The earlier you do this the better, because they have to sign it and if things are already bad they will know what you are doing and won't sign.
3. Become knowledgeable about what social support and legal resources are available. Contact your doctor for access to social services and get started with that because it takes ages to get into the system, you will need to meet many social workers and go through what is happening over and over again to different people, and must wait while they decide whether you are 'worthy' of aid or not. It is a stressful and unpleasant experience and should be

begun as soon as you know you intend to get out.

Learn about your rights in a divorce. Each country is different, so if you are resident in a country not your own don't assume you know, and DON'T rely on advice given on public forums, every case is different. Speak to the experts. You might be shocked just how little you know and how vulnerable you are. This is critical. Do not do anything until you know how to move forward in a legal way that will not come back to hurt you in court.

4. Prepare a packing list with all the essentials you need to take in case you need to leave in a hurry. Also, prepare an emergency grab bag with essentials in case you don't have time to pack and must run fast.
5. Keep all your passwords recorded in a separate location like LastPass where you only need to remember one password. Right before you leave change any of the passwords your partner knows. This is essential to protect yourself from further harm.
6. Open a secret bank account. Keep it hidden and siphon any money you can into it for your emergency survival fund. For example, if he gives you money to get your hair coloured at a salon, colour your hair yourself and put the money you would have paid to the salon into your emergency fund. It adds up.
7. Slowly stockpile necessities like toiletries and feminine hygiene products over the course of your regular grocery shops. Hide them. These items can be expensive if you

have to buy them all at once (and if you have had to run to a shelter, you will need to). It's a small thing but it makes a huge difference when you are running for you life. Box them up in advance and post them to a family member or someone you can trust so they can post them back to wherever you are when you need them.
8. If you have pets, look into emergency options for homing them if you cannot take them with you. Some social services offer foster homes for animals while you are in a shelter. Check everything. Keep notes (and hide them, I kept mine buried under the tissue paper of a pair of expensive shoes in their shoe box) because you will forget the details with everything that is going on.

Ensure you have proper carriers for cats, harnesses and leashes for dogs, any special food and medicine they need, ownership paperwork, insurance policies, etc gathered together in one place and ready to go. If you are not the legal owner, get that changed if you can. Re-register and insure them in your name. The last thing you want is to have your companion held hostage in a sick attempt to retain control over you as you try to get away.

Part V | AND THEN. YOU.

YOU ARE GOING TO BE OK

It's true. You *are* going to be ok even if right now you don't believe it. After everything you have been through, perhaps the idea of a life where you are not living in constant fear, anxiety, doubt, and fighting feelings of worthlessness and despair must seem like a fantasy.

It will take time, but you will get there. These negative thoughts, feelings and emotions are not who you are—they do not define you. They were buried there by your narcissist, poisonous seeds meant to control you and keep you paralysed in doubt while they shredded your goodness, empathy, generosity, and kind heart.

The good news is you have the power to purge the poison they have left in you. Below are simple, yet extremely effective strategies you can use to work through the harm they have done to you, to uproot the toxic weeds of their hate, and burn away the lies that choke your mind and contaminate your thoughts. These are strategies I use myself. A word of warning: It's a journey. Your healing won't happen overnight, but so long as you persist in your recovery, identify the lies as theirs, and not your truths, you will overcome.

It's important to recognise your recovery will be a day by day battle, one that will be hard in the beginning but will get easier over time. Never forget you are fighting against them, their voice, and their programming which still lingers inside you, an ugly legacy. Only you can make this stop, but you have an arsenal of weapons ready and waiting for you to aid you in your fight. You are not alone, and you are stronger than you think.

Hanlon's razor
In an earlier chapter we talked about building trust and how the most critical key in gaining the ability to trust others again is to build trust in yourself. One of the key components to building trust in yourself is opening yourself up to a subtle shift in thinking, in how you frame situations and behaviours beyond your control while still missing critical information.

This powerful tool is called Hanlon's razor. It's a simple thing, which offers a double benefit: it alleviates an enormous amount of stress plus helps you develop a more positive mindset. It's one of my most favourite methods to stop myself from spiralling into anxiety and experiencing deeply unpleasant emotions whenever ambiguity in the actions of others is present. Done often enough, this practice becomes second nature and leads to a calmer state of mind.

Hanlon's razor is a way of reasoning through unclear scenarios which helps you narrow down the most likely explanation for something to which you would otherwise assume malice. Here it is again:

Don't attribute to malice that which can be adequately explained by anything else.

In the majority of cases people are not out to get us, intentionally hurt us, or make our life worse. The trouble is for those of us either in or recovering from a narcissist's abuse, our experience with them has taught us over and over that in fact, everything they did or do to us *is* attributable to malice. This means we lose the ability to differentiate between their treatment and that of others. Eventually we only see malice in the intentions, words, and behaviour of others in every ambiguous situation. It becomes our go-to reaction and causes us an exponential amount of distress. We are trapped in a vortex of suspicion, fear, defensiveness, and self-fulfilling prophecies. We feel we have no choice but to push people away because we believe we cannot trust them.

The trouble is when we assume bad intentions two things happen right away: We immediately suffer a tsunami of unpleasant emotions like anger, resentment, bitterness, maybe even revenge—all of them ugly things, *and* we reinforce the programming the narcissist planted into us. Neither of these things contribute to your healing, instead they set you back. Way back. So this is battle number one in reclaiming yourself. Don't let the narcissist's malice make everyone else malicious.

With Hanlon's razor you gain the power of choice. Let's say you have arranged to meet a friend for lunch and they don't turn up nor do they call even after a wait of a half an hour. When you try to get hold of them, their phone is off. At this point you have two options. You can assume they are an awful, selfish person who doesn't care about you at all, and simmer in those negative feelings for the rest of the day, or you could ask yourself a question: Could there be any other reason *besides malice* which could have caused them not to turn up or be contactable for your lunch date?

If you take this step back in ambiguous situations and refuse to allow the narcissist's programming to control your thinking, you are already on your way to regaining your power over them. Perhaps you decide there are many non-malicious reasons your friend did not arrive as planned. You order your lunch, leave and get on with your day, knowing at some point you will find out the truth, all without having put yourself through the painful experience of assuming malicious intent.

Later on that evening your friend calls, and tells you why they did not make it, an emergency with their family member, a serious one. They are crying and struggling to make sense of what's happened. After you come off the call, you realise you could have chosen to be angry with them all day, but instead you did not assume they had the same negative intentions towards you as your narcissist and gave them the benefit of the doubt. You did not suffer bad feelings, and even more importantly you did not accuse an innocent person of cruelty. This is a huge step to make in building trust in both yourself and in others. Hanlon's razor is powerful, and more often than not, you will discover it is also right.

Beliefs. Thoughts. Feelings. Behaviour.

One of the most critical tools you possess to rewire your mind from the lies you have been fed is to understand how your beliefs have a powerful influence over your thoughts and behaviour. Before you met your narcissist you likely had a far different set of internalised beliefs about yourself than you do now.

Much of our unhappiness and our feelings of worthlessness and doubt in ourselves stem directly from the narrative our narcissist hammered into us. We were taught to believe their version of reality, which ensured we accepted we were the monster and they, the victim. Over time, as we internalise these lies, our truths and beliefs shrink and their narrative—their beliefs and lies about us—become our own.

What we believe informs every aspect of how we see ourselves, how we feel about ourselves, and how we act and react. If we believe we are worthless (their narrative), our behaviour will adapt accordingly to accept others treating us as if we are worthless. And so as we are treated with disrespect, our false belief in our inherent worthlessness deepens and the negative belief cycle continues to spiral ever downward, a self-perpetrating lie.

To escape this trap of false beliefs, we need to understand whatever we choose to believe about ourselves *must* and will become our reality, and what we believe sets the boundaries for our experiences. This means *we decide* what we choose to believe about ourselves. It's a choice. And if we choose to believe the lies of the narcissist, we will continue to live in that reality.

We will continue to think, feel and act in ways that align with these false beliefs.

There is only one way to stop this negative cycle, to rewrite the narrative, and shift our beliefs from their limiting, destructive lies back to the empowering and powerful truths that are rightfully ours.

The easiest way to begin is with your thoughts. These determine your reactions to all situations. They affect how you interpret an event, and drive your emotions and subconscious behaviour. If you have been told you are ugly you will choose to dress in a way to make yourself invisible, your posture will change, and you will avoid attracting attention to yourself at all costs. Or, if your narcissist convinced you that you are fat, you might restrict your diet to the point of starvation. Anorexics suffer from this false belief, sometimes to the point of death. Beliefs are powerful. They can destroy you—or you can use them as the ultimate weapon to regain your Self.

How to begin? First. Be ruthless about changing all inputs in your life from negative to positive ones. That means social media, the news, entertainment, and anything else that can reinforce the lies, paranoia, doubt, and anxiety that was your sustenance for years on end. I couldn't give up social media because of my author platform so I tried a little trick: I started liking only cat videos and cat photos and following cat pages on Instagram. Eventually my feed was packed with adorable videos and photos of cats and kittens. I just kept liking them. And now, my feed is a happy place filled with good things that make me smile. Sometimes I just walk around the house and talk about how much I love cats. I know my phone is listening so it can 'tailor' my feed to my interests, so it amuses me to know it is going to give me more photos of cats. Try it. Pick something you really like. Cupcakes, puppies, flowers, trees, gardens, whales, whatever makes you happy and will bring a smile to your lips and then go nuts liking that, following, and searching for it. Talk about what you love where your phone can hear. I promise you, you can trick the algorithm and make your social media feed a happy place if you want to.

The best part is, if you are looking at something you like, (such as kittens) which makes you feel good, you are not thinking about negative things! It turns out our mind can only give its full attention to one thought at a time so it's our choice if it's going to be kittens—or our false feelings of worthlessness. We have the power to allow what goes into our head to be positive or negative. And remember: what we consume, who we surround ourselves with, and are influenced by, inform our beliefs, feelings and actions. It's that powerful. You really are what you think.

So, let's assume you have successfully switched out negative social media and news feeds to things that make you feel good. Except, it's not going to be enough just to look at cupcakes and kittens all the time, unfortunately. You will face an inevitable vacuum of time from the negativity that is rampant (and eats up half our lives) on social media and the news.

One of the best ways to fill that extra time is to turn to learning and self-improvement or hobbies you enjoy. YouTube is crammed with everything you could ever ask for when it comes to self improvement and learning. There is going to be *something* you are curious about. Look it up. It doesn't matter how random it is, if it adds value to your life, it's good. Recently I saw a course for hoop dancing. It looked terribly fun. You get a hula hoop and learn to do moves while using the hoop, nothing fancy, just fun and a lot of smiling. Seriously, anything you want, no matter how niche, you are going to find it online. Maybe it's a new recipe, or maybe it's just trying an easy yoga class, or maybe you want to take up creative writing, or photography (if it's of kittens, let me know, I'll follow your feed). Believe in yourself. You have a gift inside you and now is the time to explore it. No more negativity. Only good things for you from now on.

Now, if you are really not sure what your gift is, or don't know what you want to try or are interested in because you have been so ground down by your narcissist, that's OK. There's an easy way to divert your thoughts that costs nothing and can eat up more time than you might imagine. Google Maps. Just start zooming in to various places in the world you are curious about and virtually visit their streets. In the beginning when I was a total wreck, I lost hours exploring remote parts of the world. You can totally immerse yourself in these places with Streetview. Plus you enjoy the added bonus of escaping to another world and leaving the confines of your own. It's refreshing, distracting, and even a little stimulating. Exploring is fun. And when you are exploring and wondering what that town on the beach in Costa Rica looks like from the street you are not thinking negative things, you are thinking about new things, learning new things. You are rewiring your mind.

Win.

Rewiring your mind by defending it from negative input and feeding it with positive inputs helps you gain new perspective, alters old thought patterns, gives you the motivation to try new things, opens new doors to experiences and relationships, sparks new ideas, promotes creativity and transforms your limiting thoughts into empowering ones. Rewiring your thoughts creates new neural pathways in the brain which creates new habits

Finally, try to stay present. Keep a gratitude journal, or at the very least take a minute in the morning when you wake to think about what you *are* grateful for. When I was at my lowest, all I could get was: I am grateful for my bed because it's really comfortable. Even if it's just one thing, it's enough. Just cultivate gratitude any way you can. It does gets easier as you shift your thought patterns, and interpret the world around you from a negative light into a positive one. Be patient with yourself. Be kind to yourself. It's a healing journey, after all. It takes time.

Breathe your way out of crisis, anxiety, and negativity in less than a minute
4-7-8 breathing is a brilliant crisis management technique I discovered on YouTube. It's a breathing exercise developed by Dr. Andrew Weil and is based on an ancient yogic technique

called pranayama. At the time, I didn't really think it could work, but I was wrong.

If you are in a place of deep crisis, try this. It won't make the crisis go away, but it will make you much calmer and grant you access to the resources you need to face it.

Begin by placing the tip of your tongue on the roof of your mouth, just behind your teeth. Keep your tongue in place throughout the practice. If it helps, you can purse your lips a bit until you get used to it.

The following cycle counts as one breath:

1. Part your lips and exhale all the air in your lungs through your mouth.
2. Close your lips and inhale through your nose as you count to four.
3. Hold that breath for the count of seven.
4. Exhale from your mouth for the count of eight.

When you inhale again, you initiate a new cycle of breath. Practice this pattern for four full breaths.

Get professional help if you have symptoms of C-PTSD
According to Wikipedia, if you have endured under the tyranny of a narcissist for a long period of time, you may suffer from the symptoms of Complex post-traumatic stress disorder (C-PTSD; also known as complex trauma disorder). This is a psychological disorder that can develop in response to prolonged, repeated experience of interpersonal trauma where one

has little or no chance of escape. Situations that involve captivity/entrapment, or a situation lacking a viable escape route for the victim or a perception of such can lead to C-PTSD-like symptoms, which can include prolonged feelings of terror, worthlessness, helplessness, and deformation of one's identity and sense of self.

Victims of narcissistic abuse have many of the symptoms of post-traumatic stress disorder, including but not limited to, the following: (Below you will find two lists. The first is a brief list for those who *might* be affected by C-PTSD followed by an in-depth list of recognised symptoms of C-PTSD).

Brief list:
- Triggers that may cause flashbacks. Recurring nightmares.
- Hyper vigilance and hyper arousal of the senses. Anxiety. Racing thoughts. Obsessive, circular thinking.
- Easily startled.
- Feeling detached from one's emotions or body. Living with numbness or a sense of unreality.
- Avoidance behaviour.
- Avoiding intimate relationships. No ability to trust.
- A deep sense of guilt or shame. Belief you are different/less than other people and not worthy.
- Unhealthy coping strategies - self-harm, eating issues, alcohol, drug, prescription meds abuse.
- Overwhelming emotions which hit without warning

In-depth list from Wikipedia, (edited for clarity and ease of reading):

- Changes in emotional regulation, including experiences such as persistent dysphoria, chronic suicidal preoccupation, self-injury, explosive and/or extremely inhibited anger, and compulsive and/or extremely inhibited sexuality.

- Variations in consciousness, such as amnesia or improved recall for traumatic events, episodes of dissociation, depersonalisation/derealisation, and reliving experiences.

- Changes in self-perception, such as a sense of helplessness or paralysis of initiative, shame, guilt and self-blame, a sense of defilement or stigma, and a sense of being completely different from other human beings (may include a sense of specialness, utter aloneness, a belief that no other person can understand, or a feeling of nonhuman identity).

- Different perceptions of the perpetrators, such as a preoccupation with the relationship with a perpetrator (including a preoccupation with revenge), an unrealistic attribution of total power to a perpetrator, idealisation or paradoxical gratitude, and acceptance of a perpetrator's belief system or rationalisations.

- Alterations in relations with others, such as isolation and withdrawal, disruption in intimate relationships, a repeated search for a rescuer (may alternate with isolation and withdrawal), persistent distrust, and repeated failures of self-protection.

- Changes in systems of meaning, such as a loss of sustaining faith and a sense of hopelessness and despair.

Treatment for C-PTSD

Talk therapy is often not the best course of treatment for C-PTSD, because the trauma is embedded deep into the autonomic system and needs to be processed from there. Therefore, alternative therapies are often best for addressing the trauma from the 'bottom up' instead of CBT analysis and talking therapies which are 'top down' methods. Some alternative therapies that can help process deep trauma are:

EMDR - eye movement desensitisation and reprocessing can help process traumatic memories. EMDR therapy involves attention to three time periods: the past, present, and future. Focus is given to past disturbing memories and related events, and current situations that cause distress, and to developing the skills and attitudes needed for positive future actions.

Sensorimotor Psychotherapy - assumes trauma can manifest as somatic symptoms, and that working with these symptoms can aid the therapeutic outcome.

Somatic Experiencing - aimed at relieving the symptoms of post-traumatic stress disorder by focusing on the client's perceived body sensations.

Internal Family Systems (IFS) Therapy - effective for the improvement of general emotional and mental well-being and to improve symptoms of trauma, phobia, panic, generalized anxiety, depression, and certain physical ailments.

Yoga & Meditation - practises have been known to help manage symptoms of both trauma and C-PTSD.

Powerful Mantras to help you heal

I am not defined by the narcissist, their feelings, moods, opinions, and behaviour.

I am worthy.

My needs, feelings, and dreams matter just as much as everyone else's.

I can trust my senses. What I see, hear, and feel is real and true.

I did what I needed to do to survive. Now I am committed to my healing journey.

I vow to be kind to myself.

My love and my heart are of incredible value and are a precious gift I will protect.

I am loved. I deserve love.

YOU ARE NOT ALONE

Two months have passed since I wrote the final words of the previous chapter. On November 1st, in the midst of the second wave of the COVID pandemic, I returned to the UK from my writing sojourn in Poland. Writing this book helped me more than I could ever have hoped. The healing journey continues and I grow stronger every day, in heart, spirit, and mind. Meanwhile, the court case drags on plagued by my once-husband's relentless need to keep his promise to leave me with nothing. I use Hanlon's razor, think positive thoughts, cultivate gratitude, am cautious of the influences I allow into my life, and keep my thoughts and beliefs focused on healthy, positive objectives.

Of course, there are days when things are overwhelming, when my lawyer has no choice but to contact me with another flaming hoop my ex has tossed into the arena for us to navigate, soaked in lies and misrepresentation. On those days, there is nothing else to do but let the horror of what I must endure wash over me. There are moments of sorrow, anger, and at times, justifiable rage, but what's the point in feeding these emotions? It only makes me feel worse, and the goal is to heal.

Exercise helps in these dark moments. So I hike, hard and fast through the English woodlands and muddy fields. I call it 'outrunning my demons'. I look at the sky, the birds, the clouds, the trees, the sunset, the moon. I don't think. I just be. Sometimes I take photos. Some are beautiful. Life is like that, even in pain, there is beauty—if you know where to look.

I won't let him win. He had that power for years. Not anymore. Now it's my turn. He can take me to court for the rest of his life if that's what he wants. I won't ever give in. Ever. I will fight him. Because he hurt me, and treated me awfully, and it's my duty to resist his malice as hard as I can. I believe justice will prevail. And you attract what you believe when your intention is pure and good.

But let's talk about you and where you are with things. You have read this far. Thank you for trusting me and being a part of my journey. My greatest hope in publishing this book is to encourage you, give you hope, strengthen your belief in yourself, validate your reality, and prove even against all the odds you can escape. That it will end and you will rise again, stronger, smarter, wiser, and more powerful than ever before.

The main difference my book has from other books about narcissistic abuse is the warning of the shock you will experience after you get out and begin to heal, of the daily battle you will face once you have exited your narcissistic abusive situation—how their lies continue to live within you, buried like a poisonous seed. That's what I want to help you with. That day-to-day fight where you need the strength to overcome what's inside you, so you don't let the lie of your trauma bond send you straight back to the place you fought so hard to escape. (Or, even worse, into the arms of another narcissist.)

So, just as I promised throughout the book. I am here. You are not alone. I am available if you need additional support in your journey out of your trauma bond and back into the immensity of your stolen power. However, I can only support a limited number of women, so places are first-come, first-served.

You can read more about my support service on my website and at the back of this book (where you'll find more details and QR codes).

I am a woman of deep empathy, introverted, sensitive, creative, positive, spiritual, and caring. All my life, I have been the one my friends have turned to for comfort and consolation in times of difficulty. Now more than ever, I believe the gifts I have been given can be put to good use. I can help you, support you, and give you the tools to cultivate the strength you need to help you find yourself again. I have been through what you are going through. All of it, and I have made it through. I am here for you, to help you heal. But only if you want it. You need to want this more than anything, because, beautiful one, you are in the fight of your life, of your heart, of your soul.

Remember, you are not alone. No matter what *they* tell you. It is a lie. It is time for the truth, and for you to live your life as you were destined to do.

Elizabeth Anne Carter

THE END OF THE STORM

It was an endless storm of confusion, anguish, denial, anger, and hurt. Always hurt.

Its fury swept over her as she huddled upon the shore, its waves cold, brutal, and intent on her destruction. She held on to nothing but the hope of its end.

Endured. Waited. Believed.

Years passed before the storm's rage lost its hunger, and with its silence—calm, clarity. Peace.

She rose, weak and raw with hope. Let it be over, she breathed. Let it be finished.

The gentle lap of soft waves touch the storm-smoothed shore, its debris long gone, cleansed by the ocean swells of her heart.

On the horizon, the soft light of a new day.

And written across the sky—hard truths and ugly lies. Neither hurt her anymore. She embraced them. Allowed them to be. Just be.

A thousand memories assemble into the pages of a book. A chronicle of time. She leafs through the hurt, the sorrow, the desperation, the hopes longed for and lost, feeling nothing but gratitude.

It was a thing that happened. A passage of time, of place.

A beginning.

An ending.

She places the book upon its shelf, where it belongs. Where it was always meant to be. It melts into the dying stars of the night.

Her heart calls to her once more.

Live. Dream. Love

She smiles and walks away.

DON'T GO THROUGH IT ALONE

If you are in a space where you feel you could benefit from one-to-one support as you work to find your feet again, or just need someone there for you who can give you a safe space to regain your balance and clear those churning thoughts and doubts from your mind, you need look no further.

I am here to help you. My greatest is wish is to support you, hear you, validate the truth of your situation, and dismantle the lies that surround you so you can connect with your power to heal, regain your connection to yourself and thrive once more. You can book a single support session, or a series of sessions. Learn more about the options available via this QR code

ABOUT THE AUTHOR

E A Carter is a Swedish-British-Canadian. She's a drinker of tea, rescuer of cats, fighter of lupus, taker of photographs, and writer of books.

The Lost Letters: The Dark World of Narcissistic Abuse was shortlisted in the 2021 Page Turner Book Award, and won a PR campaign from Palamedes PR in London.

Her debut novel *The Lost Valor of Love* is the first book in the Transcendence series and is the Gold Winner of Adult Fiction in the 2019 Wishing Shelf Book Awards, and a finalist winner in the First Novel and Historical Fiction categories in the 2019 Indie Author Network's Book of the Year Awards.

Her sequel, *The Call of Eternity*, was shortlisted in the 2020 Page Turner Awards.

The Rise of the Goddess was a finalist in the 2021 Page Turner Book Awards.

Her scifi debut *I, Cassandra* won Honorable Mention in the 9th Writer's Digest Self-Published eBook Awards (2021).

Sign up to her newsletter and enjoy her exclusive novel you can download onto any device at authoreacarter.com

Please leave your honest reviews for *The Lost Letters: The Dark World of Narcissistic Abuse* on any of these sites and help this author reach more readers!

Amazon.com

Goodreads

Amazon.co.uk

Find E A @
Instagram eacarter_author
Facebook ea.carter.author
Twitter Author_EACarter

Also @
Goodreads ea-carter
Pinterest authoreacarter

Website
authoreacarter.com

www.ingramcontent.com/pod-product-compliance
Lightning Source LLC
Chambersburg PA
CBHW071345080526
44587CB00017B/2977